BRAVERY
BEADS

BRAVERY BEADS

Helping kids be brave,
one bead at a time…

Corinne Bloom
& Darren Enkin

BRAVERY BEADS

Helping kids be brave, one bead at a time…

True stories written to inform, heal, and inspire families fighting cancer and other life challenging illnesses.

All net profits from the sales of this book will benefit the Bravery Beads Foundation, a 501(c)(3) non-profit corporation.

Darren Enkin, Co-Founder

Bravery Hearts & Bravery Beads Foundation

darren@braveryhearts.com, 305-535-9097

ISBN-10: 0615833675

ISBN-13: 978-0615833675

Cover design by Scarlett Rugers, **www.scarlettrugers.com**

Interior design and formatting by Valerie Bellamy,

www.dog-earbookdesign.com

ABOUT US

Bravery Beads and Bravery Hearts are registered trademarks and cannot be used without prior written consent.

The Bravery Beads™ program allows children with life challenging illnesses to collect special beads to commemorate each procedure or event they must endure throughout treatment.

The collection of beads gives children and families hope as well as a tangible way to share their story. Over ten-thousand children with cancer and other life challenging illnesses participate in the Bravery Beads™ program each year.

Bravery Hearts™ brand offers hip and cool fashion accessories to support bravery beads programs at participating children's hospitals. Fashionista Corinne Bloom has been designing and sourcing eclectic accessories to sell as part of our brand since 2002.

Our signature Bravery Heart Necklace has sold over 300,000 units and is still going strong. Hospital gift shops and trendy retailers love selling our jewelry as it supports their local bravery beads program and makes a meaningful addition to their stores.

ACKNOWLEDGEMENTS

The Bravery Beads Program would not be possible without the generosity of my in-laws, Molly and David Bloom.

Special thanks to:
- ♥ My beautiful wife Corinne, co-founder of Bravery Hearts and Bravery Beads.
- ♥ My three amazing children: Joa, nine; Tao, seven; and Omi, five.
- ♥ Julia and Matthew Kayton, for establishing the Elliot Albert Kayton Memorial Bravery Beads Program at Holtz Children's Hospital in Miami.
- ♥ All our friends and family in Toronto and Miami that purchase our jewelry, donate to Bravery Beads, and support us on a yearly basis.
- ♥ All our Child Life Specialist friends from across North America, who are truly amazing and too many to name.
- ♥ Kirsten McLean, CEO of Bookigee for her valuable wisdom and help with getting this project started.
- ♥ My parents, Pearl and Mel Enkin for their love and support.

- ♥ Dundas, Ontario, Canada for being the best place in the world to be raised.
- ♥ All our volunteers and retailers that have supported us over the years.
- ♥ Michael Bloom and Rita Rosenbloom for Canadian support.
- ♥ The families who have generously provided essays in support of this project.
- ♥ And most of all, the courageous kids who inspire us every day.

TABLE OF CONTENTS

THE BRAVERY BEADS PROGRAM IS UNIQUE AND SPECIAL
*because it puts a smile on a child's face and hope in
a parent's heart at a time when smiles and hope are
much needed. As an invitation into this heartfelt book of
stories, let us share our own moment of inspiration.*

❧ ❧

A HEART IS BORN

WHEN I WAS IN HIGH SCHOOL, I VOLUNTEERED FOR the Canadian Association for Disabled Skiers, teaching children with Cerebral Palsy and other disabilities to downhill ski. I remember the powerful feeling of accomplishment and pride when people showed their appreciation and thanks for the help I offered, and more so when I saw those with disabilities take on new challenges.

After university, I got a job teaching behavioral therapy to children with autism. Quickly, I realized that these were very special children. Connecting with them, making them laugh and learn, as well as seeing their progress, felt extremely gratifying.

In 2002, my then fiancé (now wife) Corinne and I were talking about finding a project that would help us give something back to the community.

We were at her parents' house one day, and she showed me a box of beaded jewelry she'd made herself. I had to admit they were impressive. Some of the wire pieces were woven into cool shapes, with beads strung in and around them. It looked like hours and hours of work, not that I had any experience with beading. The last time I'd held a bead was during arts and crafts at Camp Wahanowin (a summer camp that, ironically, my wife also attended).

As we sat on the floor examining her artistry, in walked her dad. He took a look at the beads on the ground and said, "Corinne, you spend all this time creating these things that just sit in a box. Why don't you make something useful out of your beading?"

Then he told us about this program at The Hospital for Sick Children in Toronto where he served on the board of directors. At their last board meeting, they discussed a Bead Collecting program for children with cancer in which the kids received beads to commemorate each procedure and help them track the milestones on their journey through treatment.

Corinne and I felt shivers down our spines and tears well in our eyes. The symbolic nature of this program touched us deeply and the visualization of the beads representing children warriors and what they have to endure to fight their illnesses was inspiring to us.

As we reflected on how meaningful the program sounded, we came up with the idea of designing a necklace that we could sell to raise money for the bead program. We set up a meeting at the hospital with the Women's Auxiliary to discuss the logistics of a fundraiser for the program.

Corinne and I left our first meeting at the hospital uncertain of what would become of our idea. We joked that they may have thought we were a couple of nice kids who could raise a couple hundred dollars for the program and then we would be on our way...

WRONG!

Immediately, Corinne made a trip to a local bead wholesaler. She picked out some beads, went home and, within a short while, held up a necklace and said, "Dar, what do you think of this?"

Made of multicolored glass seed beads strung on a wire with a Czech glass heart emblem, the Bravery Heart Necklace was "born" in that moment.

When it came time to sell them to help fund the Bravery Beads Program at The Hospital for Sick Children in Toronto, we found ourselves overwhelmed by the response.

Our local community loved the symbolism of "helping sick kids be brave," combined with the beauty of our Bravery Heart Necklace. Instead of buying one, women would take ten, put them in their purses, and sell them to friends or strangers. They just had to wear one to guarantee more sales.

At one time, we had over 150 women walking around Toronto with necklaces in their purses and around their necks. My phone rang off the hook with the exact same story, twenty times a day. "I was in line at the grocery store and the woman in front of me loved my necklace. So I told her it was a Bravery Heart Necklace and that I had one in my purse if she wanted to buy one. Guess what? She did!"

Corinne and I started out beading the necklaces ourselves. When the larger orders came in, we recruited her family to help. We were quite a sight at the kitchen table, with the whole gang beading and trying to keep up with the orders. The funny part was how possessive everyone became over the necklaces they made, saying things like, "look at the color distribution of my necklace! It's perfect." The party came to a crashing end when we received our first order of five-hundred necklaces!

We looked for help with production. While asking around, we discovered a vocational program for underprivileged women at Goodwill. We loved this idea because it kept our vision of giving back to the community alive and well. We paid Goodwill to assemble the necklaces for us, and they did a great job. They seemed able to produce as many necklaces as we needed, and the women at Goodwill loved the work and found it very therapeutic.

Now that we had production, we could focus on sales, ensuring our volunteers remained stocked with necklaces.

Soon after, the media came calling. Articles appeared in the Toronto Star, we were featured on the "What's Hot" list in Flare Magazine, as well as appearing on a daytime talk show and an interview on primetime news. I have to admit, it was pretty exciting.

The first milestone of our fundraiser, however, was joining the "Children's Circle of Care." The Children's Circle of Care was founded in 1995 to represent significant donors from twenty-five of North America's most prestigious children's hospitals, including The Hospital for Sick Children.

In order to be in the Circle of Care, it's necessary to donate $10,000 or more in one calendar year. I'm proud to say we've made the cut every year since we started Bravery Hearts.

We'd been selling our necklaces for around six months when we received a call from Miami Children's Hospital. They had heard of Bravery Hearts and were interested in fundraising with the necklaces, as well as starting a "bead collecting" program. Corinne and I came up with a concept that offered children's hospitals a free "bead collecting" program if they agreed to sell our necklaces to cover the costs of the beads.

After we launched the Bravery Beads Program in the United States, a chain reaction began. Hospitals called us for information on a weekly basis. Originally, we developed the program for pediatric hematology/oncology units, but eventually, we just couldn't say no to any kind of sick child, so we started making bead legends and programs for cystic fibrosis, heart/transplant patients, burns, and the NICU, just to mention a few.

The idea of giving children with life-challenging illnesses beads to commemorate each procedure endured came to us via Sharon Gove, a nurse from British Columbia. Bravery Hearts was the first organization to package a Bravery Beads Program "in a box" and offer it to children's hospitals.

The fact that we did it for free, and even donated money to our participating children's hospital foundations over and above the free beads, was a gift we also found ourselves able to give.

The Bravery Hearts program continues to expand into other hospitals and to touch many lives, reminding us of how little moments—like the one in which Corinne's dad challenged us to do something with her beads—can grow into large, life changing movements.

Thank for you sharing in our vision and for your help in giving kids around the world the hope and strength to endure.

Darren Enkin

TESTIMONIALS

"The Bravery Hearts program has been the most successful and beneficial program implemented for the hematology and oncology population. The patients and families love the program, and the staff enjoys helping kids create the visual journey through their treatment. With the ever-growing responsibilities of child life specialists, one of the most valuable aspects of Bravery Hearts is the simplicity of its implementation and low maintenance of the program. I don't think I can ever truly express how wonderful Bravery Hearts is, and how much of an impact it has had on our patients."

Becky Wimsatt, Child Life Specialist
University of Maryland Medical Center

"I have to tell you, we have a parent support group for our hematology/oncology patients, and everyone is talking about the Bravery Hearts bead recognition program. I have heard nothing but positive comments. Thanks so much for helping us get this program going for our patients."

Robert J. Wing, Director of Child Life Services
UMass Memorial Children's Medical Center

"Our kids love the beads! The program gives them something to look forward to when they come in for procedures."

Amanda Holder, Child Life Specialist

Helen DeVos Children's Hospital

"I wanted to let you know that we're delighted with our bead program already. It's really amazing to introduce it right when a child is diagnosed. Bravery Hearts has a huge impact on our young patients right from the start."

Natrisha Bayer ,Child Life Specialist

Newark Beth Israel Medical Center

"Our children absolutely love collecting their Bravery Beads, but it's a real toss up as to who loves this program more, our young patients or our volunteers who sell the Bravery Heart Necklaces that support the bead program for the children. Just today, one of our volunteers said to me, "This program is addicting!" You feel so great telling people about the foundation and the bead program. When you sell them the necklace, you see the joy they feel having purchased it, knowing they will benefit the foundation, whose mission it is to provide much needed medical care and supportive services to children who have cancer, or serious blood disorders, in our community. It is such a great feeling knowing we are part of something that does so much good and brings joy to so many. This is exactly why our foundation participates in the Bravery

Hearts Program. It is a blessing to be able to give so much joy to so many people, while being able to do so much good for children and families of our community."

Michelle O'Boyle RN, BSN, CPON, President
Kids' Cancer Foundation

"I am the child life specialist in our cystic fibrosis clinic, and I have been working hard to get each of our 148+ patients started with a Bravery Hearts necklace. Yesterday, I started necklaces for two brothers, ages 12 and 13. They both have CF and had pretty rough starts in life. They are doing very well now. I explained to them how the beads are a showcase of all they have been through, and all that they continue to do to be brave and to keep healthy. I had each of them mark on the bead legend everything they have ever been through, every procedure done. I feel it is important to recognize all their achievements, past or present. Needless to say, they each marked just about every bead on the list—and grandma confirmed it to be true.

Both boys were going to need to go down to our lab after their clinic visits to have blood work done. I told them that when they got down to the lab, they should ask the lab technicians for their "peripheral lab draw" beads to add to their necklaces.

Near the end of their clinic visit, a CF team member saw the boys, came back into the staff conference room and said,

"The boys just asked me if they needed to have blood tests, and I told them that yes, they did." Upon hearing confirmation that they did indeed need their blood tests done, one of the brothers yelled out, "YES! We get more beads!" The CF team member then said, "That bead program is a program that's working if I ever saw one!"

I just wanted to share with you what a difference your Bravery Beads program is making at our hospital. Imagine kids being excited to go get poked so they can add beads to their necklaces. Who would have ever thought? Thank you so much for all that you do."

Sincerely,

Mimi Rassi, Child Life Specialist
Helen DeVos Children's Hospital

THE HEART OF A WARRIOR

by Elaine Lambert Gay

"THE BEST AND MOST

Beautiful things in the

World cannot be seen or

Even touched—they must

Be felt with the Heart."

– Helen Keller

❧ ❧

XENA WAS BORN IN A SMALL TOWN IN PICKENS County, Alabama. When she was ten months old, she got sick with a cold. Little did we know, this would be the start of a new path for us to walk.

One day in January, Xena had a runny nose, and then the next day, she was making a wheezing sound. However, Xena, being the warrior princess she was named after, still played with her toys and did her best. The cold and wheezing sound continued all day, and progressed to the point that I called her pediatrician. The night nurse told me to take her to the hospital.

At the hospital, they gave her a breathing treatment, took an x-ray, and left us in a room. After some time, I asked if we could leave, and I was told they were waiting on the doctor to come in. She came in and looked at the x-ray, and all the doctors agreed that they wanted another opinion about Xena's heart, so they sent her to a cardiologist in Birmingham. The cardiologist ran a test and said he did not have time to get an ambulance; however, the medical staff would be waiting for Xena in ICU at Children's Hospital. She was diagnosed with dilated cardiomyopathy.

The news knocked the breath out of us, but Xena rallied

on. She stayed in the hospital in ICU. They put her on meds that made her feel practically back to normal, and soon she had that ICU unit jumping around with her. Before long, we were transferred to a regular room and placed on a daily regimen of drugs.

Xena took over the next few years. We made many visits to the doctors in Birmingham, where the results seemed to always be good. We got a little relaxed and thought she might not ever have an episode.

But on October 26, 2007, Xena got sick and, once again, we went to see her pediatrician, who then called her cardiologist. Once again, we were off to Birmingham. After doing a test in the office, I heard him say again that there wasn't time to get an ambulance, but that the staff would be waiting in the ICU at Children's Hospital. "Go!" he urged.

Xena stayed in ICU at Children's for a few days. On October 31, 2007, her cousins, aunts, and uncles all came to trick or treat. Afterward, then kept her entertained in room by playing Go Fish and other games. Little did we know, the next day our lives would change so significantly. On November 1, 2007, we were moved to UAB Medical Center in Birmingham, where they did a heart cath on Xena, and the very thing that we were hoping to avoid, happened.

On this day, we were told that Xena was going to need a heart transplant, and our world, as we knew it, changed.

Surrounded by her family, who were a great support system for all of us, we were told that Xena could not leave the hospital, because she needed medication to keep her heart pumping, and that we lived too far away. Unknowingly, the Halloween celebration in the hospital was a sign of times to come, because Thanksgiving was just around the corner.

Being Xena's mother, I stayed with her in the hospital so her father could continue to work to pay our bills. My mother also stayed close by so she could help and give me time to myself, and to help handle the everyday things. The outpouring of love from so many other people was mind blowing. Local people knew that my husband was the only one working, so they started sending us money, cards, and pictures, as well as holding multiple kinds of fundraisers. We knew hope, love, and a lot of prayers were going up in Xena's name.

Xena, the true warrior princess, had been through a lot in a short period of time. Over the next few months, she had test after test, IV's, and x-rays. She got sick one time and had to be removed from the transplant list. Filled with worry, I thought about what would happen if we missed our chance. However, we were blessed when Xena quickly got better and was put back on the list.

Thanksgiving came and our family again came to the hospital, because Xena was not able to leave the floor. The hospital allowed us to use a room down the hall for our family to have our Thanksgiving meal together. We had a nice dinner with our family of about thirty. We were truly grateful for every minute we had with one another. We made the best of it and tried to do just as we would if we were at home.

For Christmas, I put a little tree up in Xena's room and decorated her door with pictures, garland, and Christmas cards. Her room was already overflowing with cards from people all over the United States. She'd received cards from classmates, friends, family, local churches, Sunday school classes, and from people we did not even know. Time progressed and before we knew it, Christmas had arrived and the family once again came to the hospital.

We gathered in the same room we had for Thanksgiving, but once again this was not like any Christmas past. This particular year, the whole family decided to give Xena money to help out with all the bills. Nobody else in the family got anything for Christmas that year. What love we were blessed with.

Even with all the love, time still moved on, without The Call, the one we were waiting for. I was getting a little sad because I knew the chance of getting a heart more than likely would have increased during the holiday season, since more accidents occur during that time period. Now the holiday season was New Year came and passed with nothing to celebrate. We were still in the hospital, waiting.

On January 8, 2008, Xena was playing with a little girl

scheduled to have surgery on her heart the next day. They played all day long in the playroom and ran around the hospital together. They had a great time, but it was time for the little girl to have a bath, in a special soap to prepare for her surgery.

I told Xena it was time for her to have one too, and then the two of them could watch a movie together, after they'd had their baths. While Xena was having her bath, I told her how this little girl was going to have surgery the next day and about how it would be a little like what she was going to have done. She did not want to hear about it.

After their baths, as we gathered in their room to watch a movie, the nurse walked in and said, "I need to speak to you." I thought he was going to tell me that the little girl needed some rest for her big day. Instead, he said, "We have a heart for Xena." It took a minute for this to sink in. Of course I had to ask, "Are you sure?"

I called my husband, who had come after work to spend time and eat dinner with us and then gone home, an hour and half away. I was scared to death, so I got on the phone and started calling the family. Every time I said we had a heart, Xena would say, "No mother, it's the other girl, not me." She did not understand that the other girl was having a different surgery, not a heart transplant.

That was the longest night of my life because we were told that she could be in surgery as early as five a.m. The whole family made it in, but the surgery did not take place at five a.m. But at 11:30, after I had fallen asleep on the bed with her, they came to get Xena. They gave her some meds to make her goofy. When I turned to go out the door. The hall was lined with family, friends, and workers, all smiling and crying because this was the day Xena would get her new heart.

The whole family came down with us and we said the Lord's Prayer together around Xena. We prayed that God would take care of my baby and help her through this surgery. Also for God to give the doctors and nurses all that they needed to keep her safe. We additionally prayed for our donor family for their loss, even though we did not know them, yet. Nevertheless, we knew somebody had lost a loved one and they needed God's loving arms around them, too.

The surgery took about four hours. We finally got to go and see Xena in the ICU. We all lined up and washed, then two-at-a-time, we all got to go in and see her. She could not open her eyes, but one little tear slid down her face and she said, "Maw Maw." She wanted her Maw Maw, so we got her.

Just a few hours later she came off the ventilator, which is rare. She made it through the night. The next day she asked where the playroom was. You can only imagine the smiles she got when she walked in. Xena made a quick recovery and was back on the floor in a few days, running around.

This was where Xena and Mrs. Jane Love started

pulling the bravery beads that she earned through all of her procedures. They made her necklaces out of them. She loves getting her beads. They are so special to us because they tell the story of Xena's life and the events and things she has been through.

Today I think Xena has six necklaces, maybe more. We had to stay in the Birmingham area until March 1, 2008, when we got to come home. We had to go back and forth to clinic, as we still do today, but what mattered was that we were home and we got to spend the summer getting ready for the U.S. Transplant Games. Held every two years, in a different State, for people to show the world that transplant patients can compete and be as active as everyone else, this event brings people from all fifty States together to share their experiences. Xena competed that year and won a silver medal in swimming.

In April of 2009, we met our donor family, the Longs. They shared their journey with us about their son, Michael Long, who is one of God's new angels in heaven. It's been a joy to meet the Longs and to get to know them. As you can imagine, they are very sweet people.

We have learned to hug a little longer, always say, "I love you," and always say your prayers. God is good. Xena is a blessing to us. She is two years out from her transplant and enjoying life the best she can.

Elaine Gay, Mother of Xena Gay

BIG STRENGTH, LITTLE BODY

by Sandy Kennedy Erb

"HAPPY MOMENTS, PRAISE GOD.

Difficult moments, seek God.

Quiet moments, worship God.

Painful moments, trust God.

Every moment, thank God."

– Anonymous

WHEN AINSLEY ERB WAS DIAGNOSED WITH LEUKEMIA at 2½ years old, her family began the, "hospital shuffle." Her treatment was a dance filled with questions, doctor visits, hospital waiting rooms, new terminology, countless medications, frightening anesthesia, spinal taps, chemotherapy, and so much more.

Thankfully, it was eight years ago when the Erb Family received Ainsley's diagnosis. She completed her two-and-a-half years of chemotherapy in March 2007. Ten-year-old Ainsley is now CANCER FREE!

Her string of Bravery Beads is over ten feet long, showing the strength that belies that little body. While at the hospital, Ainsley loved to hang her string of beads on her I.V. pole. She loved to use her Bravery Beads to decorate it and show off all the pretty colors on her string.

It is amazing to see the impact that string of beads can have on others who see it for the first time and learn what it represents. One day, when Ainsley is old enough, she too will appreciate all she has survived and know how "Brave" she was, is, and can be!

A SOURCE OF COMFORT

by LeAnn Burnett

"LETTING GO HAS NEVER BEEN EASY,

but holding on can be as difficult.

Yet strength is measured not by holding on,

but by letting go."

— Len Santos

ON MARCH 12, 2009, I GAVE BIRTH TO A BEAUTIFUL baby boy who weighed seven pounds, two ounces and measured 21 inches long. Brantley seemed to be a normal, beautiful baby, but after an hour, he started turning blue. The nurse at St. Vincent's checked his oxygen saturation and took note of the fact that it was in the fifties. She knew that something was wrong and decided to take him to the NICU.

Brantley was in the NICU for an hour when the doctors realized there was something severely wrong with his heart and made the decision to transport him to UAB in Birmingham. There, he could get treatment from the best heart doctors. In the NICU, he was started on a medicine called prostaglandin to keep his patent ductus open. Brantley had many echoes, x-rays and other tests done while in the NICU. Doctors found out that he had pulmonary atresia, a hole in his heart, and the vessels in his heart were transverse. Although the doctors and staff were so good to us, the experience for first time parents was horrible.

As I sat in the waiting room, I was drawn to a necklace that one of the other mothers wore. I asked about it and the woman told me they were called Bravery Beads. She had gotten the necklace for her daughter, who was also very sick.

She said there were many different beads that meant different things. I asked Brantley's nurse about them and told her that I would love to have one, and so I began collecting. For every echo, x-ray, blood stick, IV, and all other procedures Brantley endured, he received different Bravery Beads.

Before his first surgery, the doctor wanted Brantley to get bigger and have a stronger heart, so we waited one week while Brantley was in the NICU. Then it was time. His surgery consisted of putting a shunt into the right side of his pulmonary artery and fixing his transverse vessels. The surgery lasted between ten and eleven hours, which seemed like days for my husband and me.

Brantley was taken to the CICU for recovery. While in the CICU, he had his good days and bad, but that was very normal given what he had been through. We spent every minute we could with him, never missing a visit. Daniel read books to Brantley while he looked up at us with those beautiful eyes of his. The nurses let us hold him and change his diapers, which were the best memories ever. Two weeks passed after the surgery and we all assumed that everything was great.

Suddenly, his saturations started dropping and the doctors couldn't bring them back up. Dr. James Kirkland, Brantley's surgeon, made the quick decision to take him into emergency surgery. This surgery lasted around fourteen hours, even longer than his first. Brantley didn't do well during the second surgery at all. He had to be put on ECMO and Dr. Kirkland had to massage his heart with his hands to keep it beating.

Dr. Kirkland was able to add another shunt on the left side of his pulmonary artery, so he could get more blood flow to his lungs. Brantley made it out of surgery, but he was even sicker than after his first procedure. After a couple of weeks, he improved and was able to have all but two of his drain tubes taken out. His stitches were removed. He was alert and in better spirits.

On Easter, which was also Brantley's two month birthday, Daniel and I came to the evening visit and were surprised to find him being extubated. This was the best Easter we could have ever had.

The next morning, I was so excited when I got to the hospital and saw him off the vent. I was able to hold him and gave him his very first bottle. I couldn't wait to tell Daniel how well he was doing. We just knew he was going to be fine and able to come home soon.

Brantley stayed off the ventilator for over twenty-four hours, until he started having complications and had to go back on. He started running a temperature, blood cultures came back positive for an infection, and the drainage from around his lungs continued to get worse. Although he was taking many different medicines and antibiotics, he didn't really seem to be getting any better.

Four days after being put back on the ventilator, Brantley's saturations again started dropping. The doctors decided to get an echo and x-ray done and noticed that he wasn't getting enough blood flow to his lungs. They took him to get a CAT scan to get a better picture of his heart. The CAT scan revealed that the right shunt put in during his first surgery had closed off, and his arteries were smaller than normal.

Brantley was taken straight to the cath lab, where they tried to put a balloon in the shunt and open it back up. This operation was very unsuccessful. Brantley was so sick before ever going into surgery, his little body just couldn't take anymore. His heart stopped beating numerous times, and the doctors had to do multiple c ompressions to get it beating again. The doctors did all that they could to save him, but he was tired and ready to go home.

Brantley passed away very peacefully in my arms, and all his pain was taken away. This was the hardest thing that Daniel and I had ever gone through. I want everyone to know that being a parent is the best thing you can ever be. Spend as much time with your children as you can, cherish them, and live every day as if it were your last.

Losing a child is by far the hardest thing anyone could ever go through, but there are things in life that do help. We pray every day, asking God to give us strength to make it through this tragedy and allow us to move on with our lives. Always keeping Brantley in our thoughts and remembering the good times we had with him helps us a lot. Daniel and I are always doing something in memory of Brantley, which seems to make life easier, like planting a Dogwood tree or making shirts to wear in the American Heart Association walk.

Daniel and I know that everything happens for a reason, we may just not understand why. We know that God will bless us again one day with another beautiful baby. We just have to keep our heads held high and have faith in the Lord.

Though Brantley lived a short life, so many people loved him. He will never be forgotten. I would like his story to be a source of comfort to families that have gone through, or are going through the same situation, reminding them that they are not alone. No matter what may happen in life, just know that it has happened for a reason and that God will not give you anything you can't handle. God Bless.

A FIERCE YOUNG DRAGON

by Shannon Kelly-Barry

"I LOVE YOU, MAMA."

"I love you more, Keeghan."

"No you don't. You love me the same, and it's a whole lot."

We used to say that to each other every day. It was this silly little game he and I started. Mike and Mackenzie do it now. I think it's their way of keeping Keeghan alive in us. A quote wouldn't really have meaning because it wasn't something that Keeghan knew, and we didn't really have any type of mantra or saying that we held tight to when he was alive.

We just held tight to each other.

"MAMA?"

"Yes, Keeghan?"

"When I grow up, I want to find a cure for cancer."

"Well then, I'm sure that is exactly what you're going to do, Buddy."

Keeghan was five years old when he told me that. I never doubted he would do it either. He was one of those kids with a quiet but fierce determination, if he said he was going to do something, he was going to do it, no matter what.

How ironic it was, five years later, when he was diagnosed with a malignant brain tumor. Not long after his diagnosis, Keeghan told me that he thought *having* cancer was going to make him better able to find a cure. It was all part of some Ultimate Plan in his mind.

Maybe it was…it's hard to say. Keeghan fought his cancer hard for over two years. He died on August 31, 2008. He was twelve years old. I like to believe that he will still find that cure—he's just doing it from somewhere else.

Along this journey with cancer, Keeghan touched so many people. Often times, it was with his wit. Others were touched by his compassion. For many, it was just his unbelievable smile! But above all, I think people were amazed and inspired by his courage.

He went through so much more than most people who live to be 80, ever would. Keeghan's sister, Maxx—in his words, his, "best friend"—says that Keeghan *did* live to be 80 years old. He did it in just twelve years.

One of the ways that Keeghan loved to show off his courage (because, after all, he was only ten years old when he was diagnosed, and liked to show off how brave he was!) was with his Bravery Beads. It was during his first week of inpatient chemotherapy at Wilford Hall, when one of the techs asked him, "Have you got your beads yet?"

"Beads?" we asked.

"You don't have beads? Let's go talk to Nikki."

She took us down the hall to meet another chemo patient, Nikki, who showed Keeghan her strand of beads, and then led him to the clinic where a nurse helped Keeghan and I go down the list of beads, and figure out how many he had already earned. By the time all of his procedures were tallied up, he had earned 56 beads! That was after only two weeks in treatment.

Over the next two years, Keeghan would rack up a grand total of 610 beads, every one with its own story. For some beads—such as TPN (being fed intravenously because he couldn't keep anything down on his own), the stories aren't very nice. The same goes for things like ER visits/ambulance rides, ICU admissions, inpatient admissions and isolation. For these events, receiving a bead was the one and only positive twist...a badge of courage for enduring what no child should ever have to endure.

But some of the beads do have better stories—not always fun, but at least more interesting! Keeghan would sometimes take his strand of beads with him to the clinic, just so that people would ask him what it was. He was then able to tell his story. Because that is what the strand is, now over 20 feet in length, his story.

Keeghan's Journey With Cancer – *told through his beads.*

Biopsy – 1

Birthday – 2 - One bead for his eleventh birthday, and another for his twelfth.

Central Line/Port Insertion – 3 - 2 ports and one PICC line.

Clinic Visit – 93 - These visits covered four hospitals— Wilford Hall Medical Center, San Antonio, TX; M.D. Anderson Cancer Center, Houston, TX; Walter Reed Army Medical Center, Washington, DC; and Children's National Medical Center, Washington, DC.

Completion of Treatment – 2 - Keeghan received one of these beads when he finished his radiation treatments, and then another when he finished his first round of chemo, when we thought (hoped?) that he was finished with cancer completely.

I'll never forget the ride home after he got his last chemo treatment in 2007. He was sitting in the front seat of the car, choosing songs on the iPod to play. He played "Shut Up!" by Simple Plan and, at the top of his lungs, sang along:

So shut up, shut up, shut up
Don't wanna hear it
Get out, get out, get out
Get out of my way
Step up, step up, step up
You'll never stop me
Nothing you say today
Is gonna bring me down.

What a beautiful sound that was! I guess maybe he should have gotten another one of these beads when the doctors took him off chemo and referred him to hospice. In my head, at least, that "completion of treatment" didn't feel like a bead earned so much as one forced…a defeat more than a win.

Dressing Changes – 15

Emergency Room/Ambulance/Unusual Occurrence – 13

Endocrinology Visits – 3 -Because Keeghan's pituitary gland was also radiated, there was concern that it would stop functioning. If this were to happen, he would have needed growth hormone shots to make him grow.

In order to establish where he was growth-wise, the doctors ordered an x-ray of one of his hands. After all the brain surgeries, hospital stays, and scans he'd had so far, this was something cool and fun! He always amazed us with his way of looking at things as an adventure.

Hair Loss/Thinning – 2 - Keeghan's hair only completely fell out once, during his first round of heavy chemo after diagnosis. The reason he has two beads is because, a couple months after the hair on his head fell out, his eyelashes and eyebrows fell out too. He thought this was hilarious.

ICU Admissions – 5

Infusion Visits – 47 - One bead for every time he had to sit in a clinic attached to an IV pole to get some type of infusion, be it chemo, antibiotics, or just fluids.

Inpatient Admission – 7

Intramuscular Injection – 9 - It's mind-boggling sometimes, thinking back on the weird things that you learn to do when your child has cancer. Things that, prior to diagnosis, you would never believe you could do, or could become normal. This bead is a good example.

When Keeghan was diagnosed, we already had orders to move from San Antonio, TX to Washington, DC (my husband, Mike, is active duty Air Force). Keeghan was severely neutropenic, meaning that his white blood cell count was very low, when we left San Antonio for the drive to DC. In an effort to boost his bone marrow and get his white blood cell count to start rising, the doctors started Keeghan on GCSF shots while he was still in the hospital. So every night while we were on the road, Mike had to give Keeghan these GCSF shots in hotel rooms.

The shots had to be given in his belly. At first, Keeghan was terrified of this. He told his primary care doctor this one evening when she came to visit him. I'll never forget what happened next.

Keeghan was lying in his hospital bed. I stood on one side of the bed, Dr. DeLaTorre on the other. Keeghan told her that he would rather take the shots in his arm than in his belly. Renee (Dr. DeLaTorre) reached over and PINCHED Keeghan's arm. He said, "Owww!" and looked at her like she'd lost her mind. Then she reached over and pinched his belly. He started to say "ow" again, and then you could see the light bulb go off in his head...the pinch in the belly didn't hurt as bad as the pinch on the arm!

He took ALL of his GCSF shots in the belly.

Isolation – 20

IV Start – 19

Last Chemo – 1 - This is another of those beads that maybe Keeghan should have received one more of, like the Completion of Treatment bead, but I just couldn't do it. He earned this bead when he finished the original protocol of chemo from M.D. Anderson, but then a few months later, we found out his tumor was returning and he had to start treatment again. He didn't complete that chemo so much as he was just taken off of it because it wasn't working. Another defeat that shouldn't be represented on his strand of beads.

Lumbar Puncture – 1 - Here is a shining example of how the Bravery Beads are a highly interpretive program. Keeghan never actually had a lumbar puncture. But because the purpose of a lumbar puncture is to draw out cerebrospinal (CS) fluid, and he had CS fluid drawn from his ventriculostomy (the drainage tube in his head after his brain surgeries) at M.D. Anderson, the nurse at Wilford Hall who gave him his first beads thought he deserved this one.

Morphine – 7 - This was one of Keeghan's favorite beads, but not for the reason you might think. He hated earning this bead, because it meant that he was having pain, but the bead itself was a pretty blue dolphin. Because he always wanted to grow up to be a marine biologist, this was a great bead for him. He wished it were for something other than getting morphine, though. Luckily, his type of cancer didn't really cause him a lot of pain. He earned these beads more from incision pain after surgeries.

Neurosurgery Clinic Visits – 5

Occupational Therapy – 15

Other Specialty Visits – 1

Physical Therapy – 43 - Keeghan started PT in San Antonio, and then later continued at the National Naval Medical Center at Bethesda. But it was at Georgetown University Hospital that he really started to love PT days. He thought his therapist, Cathy, was so cool. He especially loved the fact that she let Maxx help out.

Maxx and Keeghan were only two years apart in age, so there had never been a time in his life when Maxx wasn't around. She went to almost every PT and OT appointment with us and was his biggest cheerleader!

Whenever I think of PT appointments, I always think of this one funny thing that Keeghan always did. If Cathy showed him how to do something new, she'd give him the instructions and then ask if he understood. He would think about it for a second, nod, and then just say, "Mmm hmmmm." It was his standard response to everything with her. It always made her laugh.

Port Access – 87 - Keeghan had two different ports during his time in treatment. Each was placed in his chest, the first on the left side, just below his collarbone, and the second in the same place on the right side. To access the port for chemo or labs, a one-inch needle had to be stuck through his skin and into the port.

Try to imagine this being done to you eighty-seven times… and then try to imagine having it done when you were ten, eleven, or twelve years old. This bead should be made of solid gold as far as I'm concerned because of the amount of bravery required to go through all of that is colossal.

Radiation – 33 - One bead for the consult where he was fitted for his mask, and then 32 actual radiation treatments. The mask, made of white mesh plastic, was molded to his face. When they put him on the radiation table, the mask would then be bolted down to the table so that his head could not move.

The day they made his mask, I thought I would completely lose my mind! The mask was flat to begin with. The tech warmed it up in hot water. When Keeghan was in position on the table and ready, she put it over his face and then PUSHED it down and immediately bolted it to the table. He had to stay like that for what felt like forever to me (but was probably only a minute or two). I *knew* that, when the mask was removed, Keeghan was going to freak. I was in tears just watching! So I braced myself and prepared for the tears when she removed the mask, but instead of tears, Keeghan looked at his dad and me and said, "That was SO COOL!"

You have to love ten-year-old boys, eh?

Relapse – 1 - Sadly, some kids actually earn this bead more than once. I think once was hard enough for Keeghan. For all of us. Keeghan had a routine quarterly MRI at Walter Reed on December 19, 2007. The next day, one of the oncology fellows called to tell us that the tumor was coming back. Because it was right before Christmas, we had to wait until after the first of the year to meet with the neurosurgeon to go over the scans.

I remember Maxx sobbing in the hallway, and Keeghan trying to hold himself together to console his sister.

So much hope, dashed. So much love, helpless. Relapse is the worst word in the dictionary for the parent of a child with cancer.

Surgery – 6 - Three brain surgeries, two port insertion surgeries, and one port removal surgery.

Tests & Scans – 47 - MRI's, CT's, EEG's…the scans seemed endless!

TPN – 2

Transfusion – 11

Tube Insertion – 7

Vomit – 47 - We took a little creative license with the Bravery Beads on this one. Technically, there isn't a bead for vomiting, but Keeghan and I discussed it when he went through his first round of chemo and was puking all the time. Puking is nasty business and should have some kind of positive side. So Maxx and I went to the store and were looking for something that would make a good bead for vomiting.

What we settled on were jingle bells. Sounds weird, I know. The kids and I made jokes about the old saying that every time a bell rings an angel gets its wings. So whenever he puked, we'd say, "Keeghan's busy giving an angel its wings." We even put it into a song, humming Christmas carols. It was pretty funny—and a little disturbing.

Jingle bells, jingle bells, jingle AAAAAWWWW WWLLLLLL (insert the sound of puking here) **the way!**

Like I said, we're weird.

Hospice Visits – 3 - Darren from Bravery Hearts helped me out with this one. There was no hospice bead, but we wanted something to put on Keeghan's strand to represent the visits from his hospice doctor and nurse. Darren came up with the idea of a lion bead to represent Keeghan's amazing courage. At the time when Keeghan was referred to hospice, we thought he would have a few weeks to receive these beads. He died six days after his first hospice visit.

Bravery "B" Beads – 52 - This bead was given whenever Keeghan did (or endured) something that required bravery above and beyond the norm. Personally, I think he deserved 103,974,312,937,545,727,310,4570,975 of this one!

Two more beads added to Keeghan's strand weren't officially part of the Bravery Beads program. One was a silver charm with a shamrock on it, purchased in Northern Ireland while on his Make-A-Wish trip.

The last bead was added after Keeghan's death. It took us a while to settle on a bead to represent his final act. He conquered his cancer. Not in the way that any of us wanted, but he did beat it. Keeghan had a pretty extensive dragon collection. He loved dragons. What better to represent beating cancer than a fierce dragon, right?

So as the final bead on Keeghan's strand–the final leg of his journey—a green dragon was added.

It might seem like Keeghan's story is a sad one, and yes, for us left behind missing him, it is. But he wouldn't want people to think about him with sadness only. Through everything, he always found a reason to smile. His beads helped him do that. And as we look at the strand now, hanging on the wall for everyone to see, we smile also—remembering the courage of such an amazing boy.

Thank you, Bravery Hearts, for giving my baby a way to tell his story.

ONE OF THE FORTUNATE ONES

by Leslie and Ben Rodriguez

"YOU GAIN STRENGTH, COURAGE, AND CONFIDENCE

by every experience in which you really stop

to look fear in the face.

You are able to say to yourself, 'I lived through this...

I can take the next thing that comes along."

– Eleanor Roosevelt

IT WAS A MONDAY MORNING, AND MY FOUR-MONTH-
old daughter, Emily, developed a high fever that ranged from
102 to 104. I panicked and took her right to the pediatrician's
office, since it was her first fever (and she was my first child).
The pediatrician told us to give her Tylenol to bring the fever
down and sent us home.

On Tuesday, when her fever was still high, I brought
her back to the pediatrician. This routine happened again
on Wednesday, Thursday and Friday. Throughout the week,
Emily was diagnosed with a variety of ailments from an ear
infection to roseola, and she was given antibiotic injections
twice.

By the weekend, I brought her to the ER at our local
hospital with a high fever, a rash all over her body, bright
red lips and bloodshot eyes. After three days in the local
hospital with no definitive diagnosis, Emily was transferred to
a regional children's hospital. She was immediately evaluated
by a pediatric cardiologist upon admission and diagnosed with
Kawasaki disease, the leading cause of acquired heart disease
in children. Emily was treated with two doses of intravenous
gamma globulin (IVIG), which is the protocol for Kawasaki
disease patients.

Although the vast majority of patients who receive timely treatment recover completely, a small percentage develop cardiac complications in the form of swelling or aneurysms of the coronary arteries, which are the arteries that supply the heart muscle with blood. In hindsight, I am happy that, at the time, I didn't know anything about Kawasaki disease, nor did I have access to the Internet to learn more. As it was, in addition to the diagnosis and treatment, we dealt with a great deal of prodding and testing during our stay in the hospital.

At our local hospital, they had performed a spinal tap to test for meningitis. Holding a four-month-old still, while a doctor sticks the longest needle anyone's ever seen into her back, is not something I'd ever want to repeat. However, when the results came back, it showed potential signs of bacterial meningitis. The infectious disease doctor thought it could be a false positive due to contamination and wanted to repeat the test.

Once again, I had to watch my four-month-old receive a spinal tap. Fortunately, the results came back negative this time. After a long week of various testing and treatments, Emily was slowly improving and the cardiologist confirmed she was on the path to recovery. We were finally released from the hospital.

Once we returned home, I began to research Kawasaki disease on the Internet and realized how lucky we were that she was diagnosed early and treated. After reading stories from families whose children had Kawasaki disease but weren't diagnosed immediately and now faced ongoing challenges, I was very thankful Emily wasn't one of them.

Almost one week after being released from the hospital, she started running a low-grade fever. I called the cardiologist immediately and he assured me that, if the fever was under 101, we were probably okay. We went to Emily's first week cardiologist checkup, hoping to hear positive news. The cardiologist performed the routine echocardiogram to check the status of her heart and coronary arteries. We were horrified to learn that the initial IVIG did not fully suppress the inflammatory response of the disease. The disease was therefore still active, resulting in the development of coronary artery aneurysms. My heart dropped. This time, I knew enough to know what that meant...

Emily was readmitted to the hospital, where she spent another week receiving more IVIG, and very high-dose steroids. I kept asking myself how and why she got so sick. To this date, nobody knows what causes Kawasaki disease. I was so sad, frustrated and angry. Luckily, I have a strong family who provided a great support system that kept me focused on the positive, and on working toward getting Emily better.

Fortunately, she began responding to the additional treatment and regaining her strength. Once she was released from the hospital for the second time, she had weekly trips to undergo echocardiograms, EKGs, and blood tests to ensure her health didn't digress. Because of the relatively large size of her aneurysms, she was treated initially with an anticoagulant, Lovenox, which required twice-daily injections - which I had to administer.

That thought rattled me. I couldn't even watch when someone else gave me a shot—how would I ever be able to give my little baby two shots a day? That's when I realized that a person does what she has to do. I administered the shots for about six months before the cardiologist was comfortable with the size of her aneurysms and took her off the Lovenox.

Over time, the cardiologist visits slowed to every other week, then once a month, twice a year, and now, yearly. Emily is a happy, thriving young girl. She is one of the fortunate ones. Her coronary aneurysms still exist, but have decreased dramatically in size.

When Emily turns eight, she will undergo exercise testing to confirm that she is safe to participate in competitive sports, but her long-term prognosis appears to be very favorable. She remains on daily aspirin therapy and may have to continue with this the rest of her life—a small price to pay. We are so fortunate that Emily has come so far.

CHERISH EVERY MOMENT

by Melissa Byrd

"ONE CANNOT GET THROUGH LIFE WITHOUT PAIN,

what we can do is choose how to use

the pain life presents us."

– Bernie S. Siegel.

❄ ✳ ❄

ON DECEMBER 6, 2007, JENSEN DANIEL BYRD STARTED down a traumatic road. At just two years old, while he was playing at the McDonald's playground with friends, he stumbled and fell against a bench seat. Unable to effectively verbalize his pain, he just cried that his tummy hurt. Later, his tummy was hard to the touch, and he cried inconsolably over the pain. After exhausting other explanations, we made the trip to the emergency room. Early into the next morning, a very caring and thorough doctor, now a great friend, located a tumor larger than a grapefruit in his abdomen.

On December 9, 2007, Jensen was diagnosed with stage four, high-risk neuroblastoma. He was transferred to a local children's hospital for biopsy and began chemotherapy treatment immediately. Our lives spiraled into the bottomless pit of hell in just two short days. Words cannot describe our pain.

The initial hospital stay lasted nearly a month, leading to two rounds of chemo, and two major surgeries. In the first 72 hours of our hospital stay, I aimlessly wandered around the hospital, where I noticed a beautiful heart-shaped pendant on a colorful necklace hanging in the gift shop window. I was drawn to it, just stared at it, but I never went in. Realizing how taken I was with the necklace, my observant husband bought one for me. Later that day, he bought one for my daughter, and my mother-in-law. He was told the necklaces were a symbol of bravery and that the proceeds from the necklaces went to the Bravery Beads Program.

I proudly wear my necklace as a constant reminder of the struggles our son went through, and continues to go through. It helps me stay strong for his sake. Now, two and a half years later, I have only taken the necklace off once. In April of 2009, I took it off when our son completed his 14-month treatment protocol and was cleared of cancer. Three months later, on his first set of follow up scans, the cancer had returned with a vengeance. The necklace went back on and has not come off since.

In the course of the last 27 months of treatment, I have purchased the necklaces for friends, family, and supporters, as a symbol of our bond to push for a cure, and to ensure a long life for Jensen. I constantly receive compliments when I wear it, which in turn opens the door for discussion of childhood cancer, and the need for funding and research. I continue to spread the word about the program to new families and friends we meet along our journey.

In our initial stay at the hospital, we were also introduced to a new phase of the Bravery Beads program. For each of Jensen's procedures, tests, and aggravations, he received a new

Bravery Bead. These offered great motivation through the pain and a great distraction for our sadness. Eventually, his necklace grew to the length of a jump rope, and we still have it as a reminder of his trials and tribulations.

Since that initial diagnosis, Jensen has undergone 14 rounds of chemo, a stem cell transplant, 29 radiation treatments, three major surgeries, two central line placements, antibody therapy, multiple transfusions, sticks, and scans. He has relapsed a second time with brain involvement and is currently in treatment, requiring another two years of antibody therapy and oral chemotherapy. The relapse rate for neuroblastoma is extremely high, and he will be followed for most of his life to ensure his state of health.

Jensen's upbringing took place in hospitals; he knows no different. As a result, he makes the most of every situation and encourages all of us to do the same. He has taught us to cherish every moment, good or bad, and to never take anything for granted. He is a smart young boy and has extensive working knowledge of his health and treatments. Though he's endured more pain than most adults I know, he's always worn a smile. His smile is infectious and his personality has touched the lives of so many. All the while, the Bravery Heart necklace stands as a symbol of hope and strength for us all. In it, we have found courage to get through this trauma as a family with inexhaustible love and support.

2012: AN UPDATE

Unfortunately, Jensen passed away on August 24, 2010. He went through three tough relapses since his initial diagnosis. The final one came so suddenly, only two weeks after clear scans. By the time it was caught, there was nothing they could do. He died with us here at home, and we continue to grieve heavily every day.

The bravery heart necklaces, as I wrote before, were so special to us, and we wore them to the end. My mother-in-law and I removed ours at the viewing and laid them in the casket in Jensen's hands for burial. Just a week before his relapse was diagnosed on August 8th, we moved into a new home. My daughter's necklace was lost in the move, and she has asked for a new one several times since. I just cannot bear to get her another one. It is a painful memory of his passing, but was an amazing symbol of our love and respect for him, as well.

FOR THE WARRIOR CHILDREN

by Robyn Frook

"IT'S NOT THE YEARS IN YOUR LIFE THAT COUNT

but rather the life in your years."

– Abraham Lincoln

I'LL NEVER FORGET THAT YEAR-END BALL TOURNAMENT.
As all of the children's teams were being announced and trophies presented, our son was so excited to see his ball team get their awards. But then the microphone was shut down and the festivities came to a close, leaving our five-year-old son empty-handed, a look of disappointment so deep on his face, I needed to comfort him in my arms. He was crying because his name hadn't been called, and he didn't get a medal like the rest of his teammates. It's true, they were his teammates, and we had paid for his spot on the team that year, but he wasn't allowed to play.

You develop a way of telling your story, from beginning to end, when a new person asks you about your child's illness. We'd like to share ours with you in the same fashion we do when we introduce someone to our life, living as a family with a child who has cancer. We hope that it brings you closer to the world that we've come to know, the world which exists all over Canada and abroad, the world known to our 'Warrior' children.

Sunday, April 27, 2008 started out as any other. Our family

played out the simple routine of church and then home again s, settling into a peaceful afternoon before dinner, and evening preparations for the new work and school week, starting in the morning. My husband works shift, and just so happened to be going in for his last night shift that evening. Our whole family enjoyed a relaxing time together squeezed into (what was supposed to be) a four-man hot tub. We had not done this before and we really enjoyed lots of giggles, and fun.

As my husband went off to work, the kids and I stayed at home, enjoyed some down time. I tucked both our seven-year-old daughter and five-year-old son into bed, following the usual bedtime story. There was nothing unusual about that night; nothing was out of the ordinary. When my regular morning wakeup call came at five am, I knew it was going to be a busy morning. Our daughter had a choir concert that evening, so I had the added chore of ironing a shirt for her performance.

Our son awoke as usual, came out to the living room, and asked for his breakfast. He was my little breakfast eater, always having oatmeal and toast and sometimes even a piece of fruit, even. I vividly remember him grabbing for his TV tray as he sat anxiously on the couch, watching, "Out of the Box," awaiting his toasted English muffin with butter.

No sooner had I placed that plate in front of him and turned back toward the kitchen, than his nose started to bleed.

I quickly grabbed him some Kleenex and asked him what happened, holding the Kleenex to his nose. He said that it "just started bleeding." By this time our daughter was up and I needed to tend to her breakfast needs, so I told our little guy that he'd need to hold the Kleenex until the bleeding stopped.

I'm sure if you are a parent, you can imagine how the house was abuzz on that Monday morning. I was finishing up that ironing, getting breakfast for the second child, making lunches, getting clothes – husband walking through the door from his nightshift – I mean, I didn't have time for a nosebleed. So, when our son became more upset, crying that the nosebleed wasn't stopping, I grew frustrated, telling he needed to stop crying, crying was only making it worse.

Finally, after about 45 minutes, my husband called the local hospital. They told us that our son should be brought in and seen by a physician. Something came over me then. I undressed from my work clothes and immediately went to our son's aid. I became very panicked when I noticed that he was actually choking on the blood as it poured down his throat. Then he started to throw up the blood that had pooled in his stomach, which threw me into an emotional mode I've never experienced before. Once he was more stable, we grabbed his Buzz Lightyear face towel, put it to his nose, jumped in the car, and headed to the closest emergency room.

While there, the nosebleed finally stopped, a total of one

and a half hours after it began. The ER nurse thought he looked anemic, and we waited in a room until the doctor came in. The doctor made the decision to have his blood drawn and instructed us to wait for the results. We knew that something was up when he said, "Your son is very sick and needs to be seen by a pediatrician. I am only an emergency doctor. We've called a neighboring town, and they are awaiting your arrival."

Then we were given a cooler bag containing blood that hadn't been used, in case the new hospital needed more of our son's blood. Once at the larger center, we were whisked into a room in the ER to wait for the pediatrician. When the pediatrician came in, we went through all the events of that morning. He bombarded us with questions dating back to my pregnancy. We were completely unprepared, but followed along with the process.

The pediatrician started pointing out the bruises on our little boy's legs and asked if he was bruised like this often. Always, we said. But we live in the bush and our property is full of adventure for five-year-old boys. That adventure came with cuts and scrapes and typical little boy behavior, including bruises from falling and knocking into things. The doctor noticed other bruising, though, that we never noticed. Little bruises, like where his shoulder blades applied pressure on his back. And we were told that he had a heart murmur and an enlarged spleen.

By this time, my mother, who has been a nurse for over thirty years, was at the emergency department. I had called her because I knew that we were going to need help with our daughter's choir recital that night. Because of her experience, my mother was way ahead of the game; however, my husband and I were not. We were told that our son was in dire need of a blood transfusion, and since he was AB- (the rarest blood type), they didn't stock a supply in the hospital, as the demand was not great enough. So, off we went to hospital number three, Children's Hospital of Western Ontario [CHWO].

CHWO was also awaiting our arrival. We were placed in a ward room, where we waited for the resident to come and speak with us. His name was Roman and he was great. He was also the first professional that I asked, "What do you think it is?" His reply was vague. He said that he didn't want to say because he didn't want to worry me.

We once again went through the drill of questions. They took more blood and this time they started an IV. Once the fourth IV attempt was successful, our little man was playing and content on this gurney. So we just waited for the chief resident to come talk to us.

As this woman came to our son's bedside and closed the curtains, I'll never forget the positioning of the three of us, my husband at the foot of the bed, me at the side, and our son playing in it. In a 'matter-of-fact' tone, like one would hear from a teacher giving out homework assignments, these words were spoken, "I'm sorry, but your son is very sick. He has either leukemia or lymphoma, and his diagnosis is to be confirmed tomorrow following a bone marrow aspiration."

Okay, pardon? Come again? I went hot from head to toe. I froze and felt as if my feet were melted into the floor. My husband leaned over and grabbed the edge of the bed. And there was our happy son, still playing on his gurney, not realizing what was just said.

And so our life as we know it now, has just passed the one year anniversary mark. Our son's diagnosis of acute lymphoblastic leukemia (ALL) was confirmed on Tuesday, April 29, 2008. After a two week stay in the hospital, and four weeks at Ronald McDonald House in London, ON, we were finally able to go home and commute to CHWO for his treatment. I could go into all the medical details about the phases and such, but that's not the intent of this story. We would like this story to be a legacy to him and all the Warriors fighting this disease.

Our family was thrown into a crash course on leukemia, and we believe that we have not only learned from our own experience, but we continue to learn and be influenced by the experiences of others.

There are many wonderful organizations that get donations and raise funds to help these cancer children and their families during this most difficult of life journeys. I know our son's experience benefited from the positive influences of, the Pediatric Oncologists, Therapeutic Ollie the Clown, art therapy, cRaZy nurses, Caringbridge, and Bravery Beads. See, once you take away all this fun stuff, you're left with children in a pediatric oncology ward in a hospital. Not a place you'd want to spend your childhood.

It's amazing how our son is marking his journey. When people see the strands of Bravery Beads, they are flabbergasted, to say the least.

When you say, "He had another spinal tap," or, "He cried a lot when his port had to be accessed." You don't tend to add all those times up together, but that's what the Bravery Beads do. They add up all of his leukemia experiences that earned him a bead. All the pokes, tube inserts, emergency visits, blood transfusions, spinal taps, bone marrow aspirations, platelet transfusions, hair loss, NPOs—all of these are compiled into strands of beads for him to look at and see just how brave he was.

Our son is now six years old. His hair has grown back, he has lost all of the excess weight from steroids, and he's a typical senior kindergartener at school. He is one year into a three-year treatment plan, actively on chemo every day, and living life to his full potential. He has had some minor side effects from the chemo. Only time will tell if the minor will produce major, as he is a young boy in a time of development, all the while getting toxic medicines put in his body to rid him of this disease and prolong his life.

Oh, and about last year's ball tournament: The coach's wife saw the events unfold and watched Dalan's heart break in two. Within seconds, someone turned the microphone back on. There was a hushed silence, and then, "There is now a very special medal for our one-of-a-kind T-Baller, Dalan Frook. Dalan, will you please come up and get your team medal."

It was the first time in months that I saw that look of excitement come over his face—you know the one. The one that pulls on your heartstrings so deep that it melts your heart...

To him and all the Warrior children, we would like you to know that you are our superheroes. You are gifts to be treasured and stories to be told. Some people will be influenced by your journey and others scared to listen. Know that you are special gifts to us, and to the world.

A REMINDER OF OUR SWEET ANGEL

by Danielle Lambert

"SOME PEOPLE ONLY DREAM OF ANGELS,

we got to hold one in our arms."

— Author Unknown

❧ ❧

ON SEPTEMBER 8, 2004, OUR DAUGHTER, KAMRYN
Mackenzie Lambert, was diagnosed with acute lymphoblastic
leukemia. It was a week after she started first grade and also
the first week of soccer practice, a sport in which she was a
superstar. At the first practice, Kamryn felt sick and dizzy and
looked very pale and very tired. She had also been bruising
very easily, and not just regular bruises, but big lumps and
purple blotches. Something we had never seen before. We
thought that maybe she was anemic, so we made a doctor's
appointment. We could never have imagined what was causing
our little girl to feel so weak.

The next day at the doctor's office, they did a finger prick
blood test. The doctor's next words still make my stomach
drop and my heart sink, when I think about them. "Take her
to the hospital now. Don't go home, don't stop anywhere, take
her now." My husband met me at the first hospital, where we
waited for what seemed like an eternity to find out what was
wrong. Then, hours later, a doctor pulled my husband into a
room and told him those unforgettable words, "Your daughter
has leukemia."

We were transferred to University of Maryland Hospital
to have Kamryn admitted and to find out exactly what type

of leukemia she had. For the next week, it was a whirlwind of pain and emotion for Kamryn, my husband, and our family. The good news was that she was diagnosed with ALL, acute lymphoblastic leukemia, the most common, most curable type of childhood leukemia. The bad news was, she would have to go through three years of chemotherapy and a variety of other medicines to overcome it.

The first thirty days were the most trying and the most painful. Kamryn lost all of what little weight she had, and all her muscle mass. She was taking high strength steroids and chemo, which caused her to develop mouth and throat sores. She had terrible muscle pains and vomited constantly. My husband had to sleep on the floor in her room for that month, because leaving her side was not an option. On the thirty day, also her 6th birthday, she was in remission. We knew that we still had a very long way to go, but with her spirit and strength, we knew we could get her through, because she was, in turn, getting us through.

For the next year-and-a-half, we were in and out of the hospital every week for treatments, inpatient stays, and count checks. What started to happen was amazing. Our quiet, shy little girl became a strong, sociable, and mature person. Kamryn took pride in helping new kids get comfortable with the needles, and the shots. She sat with the little ones while they got their port accessed and hold their hands if they were scared.

Kamryn loved to help the nurses on the floor and loved feeling like she was not only a patient, but also a part of the hospital family. Every nurse knew her name. She hung like a big girl, and kept everyone smiling and laughing.

She learned how to live again. She was feeling healthy, getting her muscles back. She started taking dance lessons, even started cheerleading. Everything was going smoothly, every checkup was great, every count check remarkable, but everything was about to change...again.

In February of 2006, Kamryn relapsed. All of the strong, brave, positive energy that she had possessed was gone when we told her, "Yes, sweetie, you did everything you were supposed to do, but it just didn't work." We knew that this time around was going to be different, with different medicine, stronger chemo, and the addition of radiation.

Slowly Kamryn's spirits started to rise again and her strength to beat her illness returned. I remember the day her daddy brought her home from treatment and she had this beautiful necklace around her neck. She told me that she got it for being brave. I cried. To me, she was the epitome of bravery. She said, Becky, her child life friend, told her that she could get these necklaces for being brave. She loved the idea that when you bought one of those beautiful Bravery Heart necklaces, you were giving money to help sick children like her. She was so proud.

The next week, my husband bought one for me. The next month, we bought them for each of our mothers. For three years, we saw the remarkable bravery that children in the hospital show. The overwhelming strength these kids exhibit, trying to conquer their disease, or disability, is indescribable. Being able to wear a necklace to honor these brave-hearted children has meant the world to us. Even more, it showed Kamryn how truly proud we were of her. Every time I put it on, she knew it was for her bravery. That's a smile that I will never forget.

Sadly, on September 3, 2007, after three years of bravely battling her illness, Kamryn passed away after a month-long fight, in the ICU. When we had to go through the heart-wrenching details of her arrangements, we knew there was one thing she had to take with her. She had to take her Bravery Heart Necklace. We wanted her and everyone else to see, the symbol of her bravery. Her Bravery Heart Necklace would help us all remember how brave she had been.

Since then, we have bought other necklaces for our nieces. None of them are sick, none of them are disabled, but they know that this necklace is a connection to the cousin they lost. The necklace makes them feel close to Kamryn, and they feel that they are now honoring her bravery as well.

Since the Bravery Heart Necklace held such deep meaning for Kamryn, my husband, and me, my husband and I decided to honor our daughter, by getting the Bravery Heart Necklace tattooed on our wrists, as a symbol of how proud we will always be of her bravery, The pain was tremendous, but I knew that it was nothing compared to the pain that Kamryn, and all of the kids battling illnesses feel every day. I needed to be brave just like them. In addition to being a reminder of our sweet angel, my tattoo gives me the opportunity to share my story of Kamryn and the Bravery Hearts. It is a whole new way of opening people up to this wonderful program and to keep Kamryn's story alive.

Never have I treasured a piece of jewelry so much, because it was never just a piece of jewelry to Kamryn. She was so honored and felt so special that someone made a necklace to honor her bravery. I can never thank this program enough for the very special memories and feelings it has give Kamryn and our family.

MOTHER'S INTUITION

by Joanne Roderick Lee

"BEING DEEPLY LOVED BY SOMEONE GIVES YOU

strength, while loving someone deeply gives you courage."

– Lao Tzu

FEBRUARY 1ST, 2006. THE DATE WILL BE ETCHED IN MY mind forever. It started out pretty normal, except that Samantha, then six years old, wasn't feeling well and stayed home from school. I dropped three-year-old Matthew off at preschool and went to the school to help out in Sam's classroom, while a friend of mine watched Sam. On the way home, I called our pediatrician, though I am not quite sure why, Sam didn't have a fever just a tummy ache. I guess you could call it mother's intuition…something just didn't feel right.

I took Sam in and told Dr. J. she had a tummy ache and I was concerned she may be coming down with something. I talked about a couple of headaches that woke her up the previous week. The doc said that a child should not be awakened by a headache and ordered a standard CBC. When the blood test came back, the results did not look good. Samantha's RBC and WBC were fine, but her platelets (the part of the blood that takes care of clotting) were very low. She immediately sent us to Tampa General. St. Joseph's ER was very busy.

Tampa General was pretty busy too, and we were there for many hours before we saw anyone. I had an awful feeling about this whole thing, yet I tried to keep everything light with Samantha. She is a smart kid. Even though she was just six, she didn't miss a trick. She was upset about missing cheerleading practice because we had to wait so long!

When the ER doctor told Sam to go pick a toy out of the toy chest, and then asked me to sit down, I knew we were in trouble. He also had invited a fellow doctor in. I looked out the window into the hallway where Sam was. There were many people looking at me. I knew before he even told me, I knew it was really bad news. He said Samantha had leukemia and that we would have to go over to St. Joseph's because they had a children's cancer ward. Tampa General was not equipped to treat her. He said St. Joes was holding a bed for her on the children's cancer floor and that we needed to get over there right away.

I am not sure how I drove there, but we made it. It was a Wednesday night. Her treatment started less than two days later, after a medi-port was inserted into her chest. That was on Friday, February 3rd. Saturday was pretty normal, if you want to call it that, pretty much uneventful.

On Sunday, we started a whole new nightmare. Samantha collapsed early Sunday morning when she got up to go to the bathroom. She blew a major vessel in her brain. Her brain was bleeding. Everything was shutting down and they couldn't get a line in her. The neurosurgeon told us her platelets were too low, and she may not make it through surgery, but if they waited to get the platelets in her, she would die. He said her only chance would be to operate right away and try to stop the bleeding. He had tears in his eyes.

Sunday, February 5th was by far the scariest day of our lives. At that point, the cancer that had consumed our thoughts, Wednesday no longer crossed our minds. Our baby girl could die of a massive stroke? She was only six years old. How could this happen?

It seemed like she was in surgery forever, but Dr. GP finally emerged, telling us she made it through. The next few days were heartbreaking and so very scary. I think it was a couple of days later when she was able to squeeze the doc's hand and move her foot. He told us he thought she would eventually fully recover from the stroke. Thank God!

Samantha continued to receive her chemo while in the PICU. A physical therapist came in and worked with her, even though she was completely out of it. When she finally returned to the cancer floor, her physical and occupational therapy really began.

PT and OT were intense. Samantha felt so sick and was so weak. It was so hard to watch her try to walk while they held her up, to try to pick up small objects with her hands. Things she once found so easy to do, she now had to concentrate and practice over and over again to accomplish. As heartbreaking as it was to watch, it must have been terrifying for her to experience.

Half of her hair was shaved off and she had a big ugly scar with staples. The rest of her long beautiful hair, which was in a knot from lying in bed for over a week, started falling out. A haircut was definitely in order. Despite the haircut, it did not look good, but it was to fall out completely soon enough anyway—three times over the next two years.

Samantha couldn't walk without assistance for quite a while. She was so sick from the chemotherapy. She received it by mouth, into her medi-port, and directly into her spine. In addition to enduring intense bone pain and constant headaches, the steroids messed with her mind and caused her to gain a lot of weight. The steroids ripped apart her stomach and made our once cheerful child, incredibly miserable and sad.

Over the next two years, she was in and out of the hospital often for chemo, fever, and unexplained pain. However, throughout it all, there were glimmers of the old Sam. We longed for the days where she felt well enough to smile and laugh. We cherished those moments, sometimes waiting for days to see a smile. But seeing them made those two years bearable.

St. Joe's did not have the Bravery Beads program when Sam started treatment in 2006. We inquired about the program many times to our Child Life department, but nothing. Then, ironically on the day Samantha's last spinal tap for chemo (in 2008), she received her first Bravery Bead.

She was so incredibly happy that the program had finally begun at our hospital and would be there for other kids. We started selling Bravery Heart necklaces to help support the Bravery Beads program at St. Joseph's, back in the summer of 2007. Sam decided to donate her commission to local childhood cancer organizations. The day she told me she'd like to donate back to organizations that helped us on our journey was a proud day for me. Wow, she gets "it," I thought.

So you see, some very good things came out of this nightmare. Samantha, and the rest of the members of our family, learned many people —friends, family, and complete strangers–loved us, unconditionally. Because of the outpouring of love we received, Samantha learned that giving was as good as receiving, and in a lot of cases, even better. She has learned that she is a very strong young lady. She has not only been through more than most adults, she has become a better person because of her experiences. She is healthy, happy and is currently two years post-treatment. In three years, Samantha will be considered CURED!

A SEVEN-YEAR-OLD HERO

by Charlean Favela

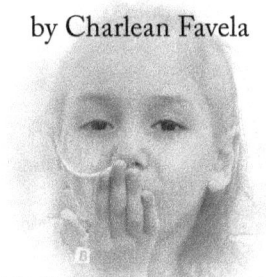

"WE ARE ALL ORDINARY. WE ARE ALL SPECTACULAR.

We are all shy. We are all bold.

We are all heroes. We are all helpless.

It just depends on the day."

– Brad Meltzer

❧ ❦

FIVE YEARS OLD AND FULL OF ENERGY, HER LIFE WAS about playing soccer, the thing she lived for most. Then the day came when her little dreams crashed down around her and she didn't understand why she couldn't play anymore. That would be the day she was told she had cancer. Her life was about to change.

My daughter Leilani was five years old when she was diagnosed with Wilms' Tumor (nephroblastoma), a form of kidney cancer. You never imagine your child having cancer, especially at such a young age. We were very honest with her. She wanted to know everything. I never kept anything from her.

Leilani had surgery to remove her left kidney along with the tumor. She then completed her treatment with chemotherapy. She turned six years old shortly after. She was happy to go back to school with her friends. Then the bad news came again. Not even three months after completing treatment, her cancer was back. She was re-diagnosed, meaning she had a relapse. This meant another surgery in the same place, high-risk chemotherapy, and radiation. Her life changed once again.

Her appearance changed drastically, going from olive-colored skin to pale white, from long hair to bald, not one hair left on her body. Even her teeth were affected. She had a feeding tube put in to help her maintain and gain back the weight she'd drastically lost. But not once was her spirit affected. She smiled, even while in pain and made sure everyone around her was smiling, not feeling sorry for her. People don't realize the depths of treatment children like my daughter go through, yet they always stay so positive.

As a mother, the day my child was diagnosed with cancer was the worst day of my life. I knew something was wrong with her, but never imagined I would hear that word. I fell apart and I cried for a very long time. As a single mother, I didn't know what I was going to do.

I truly believe that Leilani was strong for me. I don't think I would have been able to get through it without her being so positive, which is sad, because she had the cancer not me. She never asked for anything, or wanted anything. She was staying strong for me. I stopped working to be at her side every day. I was so scared of losing her.

When her treatment was over, she said her cancer was coming back. Honestly, at five years old, I thought she was crazy. A few months went by and we celebrated her six birthday. Sadly, my nightmare had just begun. We were told her cancer had come back and no one knew why. This little girl knew, she felt something was wrong, I wish I had listened to her. My heart broke once again, and it tore my family apart.

You would think, when someone, especially a loved one, a child, is sick, it would bring a family together. Unfortunately, that is not always the case. My twelve-year-old son, Damien, could not handle seeing his sister sick all of the time, so he moved away and their relationship is not what it used to be.

Leilani and I recently moved and my son decided he would not move back in with us. After losing his Nana to breast cancer, as well as his grandfather, all within the time Leilani was diagnosed, he said he couldn't be around his little sister in case she died one day like they did. They used to be best friends. It breaks my heart every day that they barely speak to one another now. Leilani feels like he left because she was sick, and he feels like he already lost her.

Cancer not only affects the person fighting the crazy disease, it also affects their loved ones. Especially siblings, who get lost in the madness and don't always know how to deal with it. I have hope that one day my son will come around and be there for his little sister. But in the meantime, he is still just a child and needs to live life as a child.

Leilani has grown and matured faster than most kids. I made sure, the second time around, treatment would be a lot easier. We learned how to replace our fears and our many tears, and turn them into laughter. Her relapse resulted in a harder treatment, but Leilani always laughed. She always made everyone laugh. That is who she is, even today.

People say that things happen for a reason. I have learned that to be true. I have learned more about life from my now, seven-year-old daughter, than I could have ever imagined. I might be broke and have nothing left, but I still have her, and that is all that matters. She is my life and she fought hard and won, twice. Not all families are as lucky as we are. At the age of seven, she is finally done with her treatment. Soon she will have her port removed in the hope her battle is over.

We have become a family in the hospital. Children, of all different ages, have become friends and understand one another. They may appear to be different to people outside of the hospital, but to each other, they are family.

Their beads tell a story of their life while in treatment. Some may have more beads than others, but they all tell their individual story. Leilani's beads tell of every surgery, every chemotherapy drug, antibiotic, blood transfusion and fever. Her many hospital stays and sicknesses, her blood being drawn, port access, being brave, and the nose tube placement she had every month to keep being able to play and have fun. The list goes on and on. But it's her story, of how her life has changed. It is also something she cherishes and uses to remember her fight–not only once, but twice. Her Bravery Beads, to her, are what make her.

She says she wants to be a doctor and a teacher like her oncologist, Dr. Singer. She will always remember what she has gone through, in those two years of her life, and her beads will always remind her. She has the strand hanging on her IV pole at home, and she calls it her friend. The beads give her courage and hope for a better life.

As her mother, I hope her Bravery Beads encourage her to fulfill her dream of one day helping other children, like herself and her dear friends. I have faith and hope she will do just that. She is, and will always be, my hero.

FINDING THE SILVER LINING

by Cheryl, Dan and Bryce Gavin

"FROM ONE BASKETBALL PLAYER TO ANOTHER:

Rest In Peace, Vanilla Double G."

– Juwan Howard

I AM WRITING TO SHARE THE STORY OF MY SON, KYLE. Our first born, Kyle arrived January 15, 1996, on my husband's birthday. A true sports fanatic, from the age of about seven, he would watch Sports Center instead of cartoons.

He was also such a kind person. When his brother Bryce's baseball team went on the field to practice, Kyle would go out there and help them and teach them all he could. The adults used to call Kyle, "The Commish," and as he started growing, his friends in school called him, "Gentle Giant," since he was about 5'10" and weighed about 160 lbs. by age twelve.

Kyle played football, basketball, and baseball. He loved all sports, but when he turned twelve, he started to really focus on basketball. He made the team for the AAU Shamrocks. That was probably his proudest moment. He played in lots of tournaments where the other parents laughed, because no matter where they played, Kyle had a crowd of family there to watch. They called us his entourage.

Kyle was planning to attend St. Peter Marian for seventh grade, in August 2008. He always got straight A's in school. He was a smart kid when he applied himself.

In sixth grade, he asked his teacher to please start calling him by his new nickname, "Vanilla Double G." He was probably the only child of this generation to know every single word to, "Ice Ice Baby," by Vanilla Ice. The Double G stood for Gentle Giant. The teacher laughed at the thought, but when there were no other kids around, she called him by his new nickname and he got so excited.

Kyle taught his brother so much. Not just about sports, but he taught Bryce how to be a good person, how to make the right decisions, and how to be a good friend. Kyle had a heart of gold. I remember when he was about ten years old his best friend Mike called, crying, to tell him that his cat had passed away. Kyle and Mike talked for about a half hour, and cried together. I was so amazed that two young boys were so compassionate and caring.

On July 5, 2008, Kyle began to vomit uncontrollably. We rushed him to the emergency room, where he was diagnosed with pneumonia and we were sent on our way. Kyle was still not himself on Monday, so I called his pediatrician and he was seen the next day. After a very rough night, we ended up at the ER at UMASS on Wednesday, for over twelve hours. After every test imaginable, from ultrasounds to x-rays, nothing was found. But his blood tests revealed a high white blood count, meaning there was an infection somewhere.

At 10 pm, Kyle turned to me and asked to go home. Though the doctors did not want us to go, I decided I would take him home and return the next morning if he was not better. He just wanted to sleep in his own bed at that point.

Kyle awakened me at 1:30 in the morning, and he told me his belly was really hurting. I gave him a blue freeze pop and brought him into my bed where the air conditioner was. I slept on the floor while he slept in my bed, and I will always remember Kyle asking me over and over again, "Are you sure, Mom? Are you sure?" I told him, "Of course I'm sure. Just try to get some rest."

The next morning, we woke to Kyle hitting the floor. He got up to go to the bathroom and just fell over. As my husband, my ten-year-old son, and I tried to talk to Kyle, we realized he was mumbling. At first, we thought he was still asleep. But after a minute, we saw him holding his right arm and trying to get it to move, but he couldn't move it.

Immediately, I dialed 911. When the EMTs arrived, they asked questions, wondering if Kyle had taken any medications. They rushed him into the ambulance, and I rode in the front, as my husband and Bryce followed. When we arrived at the ER again, a nurse named Jennifer recognized us immediately from the night before. They brought Kyle into the room, and although he was alert, he was slowly losing his abilities.

They rushed him in for a CAT scan, and then came out and told my husband and I that he had a mass in his brain. They were calling in technicians to figure out what it was and what to do. After many tests and many doctors, they brought us to a room in the PICU to meet with the doctors. They told us that Kyle had a mass and that, if it was a tumor, it was inoperable due to the location. They were going to do a biopsy later that night.

We waited with many family members and friends, packed in the hallways and waiting room. Then the doctors came and told us that Kyle was taking a turn for the worse and they were going to do the biopsy immediately. They took him about 3:30 pm, and we were told the surgery would take a few hours. As the waiting room grew more and more full, there was still no word. The waiting seemed like a lifetime.

Then around 10:30 pm, the neurosurgeon came out and told us that our child would not live more than a week. Kyle had a rare disease called Weston Hurst disease or acute hemorrhagic leukoencephalitis. Basically, it's a viral infection that attacks the central nervous system. This is so rare that there have only been about a hundred cases reported since 1941. There is no cause, and worst of all, no cure. It was like an out of body experience.

I think I was the first one to collapse, then my husband, soon after. How could this be? How could such a healthy, lively young boy get this disease? But we would never know the answers, as the doctors don't even have all the answers.

We spent the next five days living in the PICU. The staff

was so amazing. They kept us updated and tried so hard to treat this disease aggressively. On the Saturday, they put a bunch of wires on Kyle's head to read his brain activity. My husband and I took turns sleeping in his room, and he seemed to be doing okay. Then on the Tuesday, after a long night sleeping in the PICU again, I went home after my husband arrived to shower. That's when I got the call. They tried to put a central line in Kyle's chest to do the plasmapharesis and his chest collapsed.

This was the last hope we had. There was nothing else that could be done. Kyle lost a lot of blood. They stabilized him. Then we were brought into a room with Dr. Bateman and Dr. Laura Lewandowski, and we were told that there was nothing left to try. Kyle's brain was no longer functioning.

So, my husband, Dan, and I had to make a decision. One that no parent should ever have to make. Do we keep our son alive on machines for us, or do we take him off the meds and let him go in peace? We decided we could not be selfish. Kyle would not want to live like this.

So, we brought our entire family in the room and took him off the meds. Our only concern was that Kyle not be in any pain. The doctors kept giving him morphine to make sure he was comfortable. After taking him off the meds, he continued to fight, although his brain showed no activity. Dr. Bateman and Dr. Laura never left our side. Kyle passed away that night at 9:44 pm.

Our lives would never be the same. July 15, 2008 was the date. So, needless to say, the 15th of every month, being both his birth and date of death, presents a struggle. I could never thank the staff enough at PICU. They were so very amazing. They are such a dedicated team. They never left our sides.

It has been a very difficult journey since Kyle has passed away. We have done many support groups and really just cried a lot. We will sit in his room, as a family of three, and cry together. My husband stated at the hospital, when we found out Kyle would not make it, that this would not break our family, and I think that was our determination.

I feel like my heart has been ripped out of my chest and can never be repaired. It has now been ten months and fourteen days since Kyle left us, and it feels like yesterday. It's almost like time stands still for us, and moves on for everyone else. Every moment is a struggle, but we get up each day for our son Bryce.

Our memories of Kyle also help. Having no regrets is what's important. Kyle knew we loved him and supported him in all he accomplished in his twelve short years. And honestly, I am glad we had the opportunity to say goodbye. Many others don't have that chance.

Basically, we have tried to find the silver lining. After attending all these groups, I have realized that no two people cope the same way. No two situations are the same. Nobody can tell you how to feel and what to do next. I am a different person now than I was before July 15, 2008. Whether I like this person or not, it's who I am.

Many people don't realize that it changes your entire persona. Some days, I can talk about Kyle for hours and be okay. Other days, I think of Kyle and can't stop weeping. People tell you it gets easier with time, but I have not seen that at all. I think the first year is absolutely the most difficult. Then we'll see from there. I just can't imagine it being easy. Losing a child is the worst pain one can ever endure. But, with support from family, you can make it through.

BRAVERY BEADS FOR BABEC

by Bernadette Chapman

"LOTS OF PEOPLE TALK TO ANIMALS...

Not very many listen, though...

That's the problem."

— Benjamin Hoff, The Tao of Pooh

I KNOW WHY IT HAS TAKEN ME SO LONG TO WRITE down Sadie's story. Even stories with happy middles (because we thankfully do not have an ending yet) are difficult when you have to return to the worst days of your lives. It's not a sad story at all. It was just challenging one to get through.

So the story begins: Gary and I decided to finally have a baby, after two years of marriage, but having known each other for over fifteen years. I still have the fortune cookie from the day I found out I was pregnant, "A cheerful message is on its way to you." Overall, the pregnancy went well. We spent the months adding a big closet to the new baby's room, reading "What to Expect When You're Expecting," and sweetly arguing over names.

May 29, 1996, our baby girl arrived, kicking and screaming, and we couldn't have been happier. She was born roughly two weeks early (advance warning of her impatience) with a slight heart murmur, but nothing alarming. After a couple of days in the hospital, we went home.

As most of you remember, with the first child, you are constantly running back and forth to the doctor for every cross-eyed glance. On Sadie's ninth day, the doctor could still heard the heart murmur, so we ran down the street to

University of Alabama at Birmingham, to check it out. Still, no worries, we just needed to get a little medicine to close up the valve and we'd be on our way.

That was the day the earth spun out from under us.

Sadie was diagnosed with hypo-plastic left ventricle, which, to me, meant she didn't have the major pumping part of her heart, so how could she live? Dr. Bennett Pearce explained, people survive this basically by re-wiring/re-routing the veins and arteries (my words, not his).

Sadie had several caths until she was eight months old, when she went in for the Fontan procedure, and came out fine. We then decided to monitor her until we all felt it was the opportune time for the Glen procedure, which happened when she was eight years old. During this hospital stay, the Bravery Beads were introduced. They'd end up giving Sadie a sense of what she went through.

The surgery was a great success. Sadie and her heart are doing better than anyone could have prayed for. But after her surgery, she became very depressed, an expected side effect of open-heart surgery in adults. This was a very frustrating time for all of us as we tried to figure out what was wrong and how to fix it.

One day, we took her to the Birmingham Zoo, where she became aware of Babec the Gorilla. Babec had also had heart surgery. Heart disease is very common in Silverback

Gorillas in captivity, they don't know why. Sadie instantly felt a connection with this 400 pound furry guy. She wanted to meet him, and no one was going to stop her.

After finally convincing her that she couldn't just walk out into the cage area, she decided to write a letter to the zoo about herself and her desire to meet Babec. Sadie wanted to give him his own set Bravery Beads, because he had gone through many of the same procedures she and the other kids had, at the hospital. Several weeks later, we got a call from Marsha, the mammal curator, inviting Sadie to meet Babec. Of course, we all said, YES.

One sunny spring day, Sadie came face-to-face with her new friend and presented him Bravery Beads. (There was a metal gate between them.) She watched as he ate carrots and strawberries and learned his favorite snack is Cheez-its.

Sadie has continued to champion Bravery Beads and the Red Dress campaign, and she is in great health.

NOT JUST A NECKLACE

by Jennifer and Terry Deerman

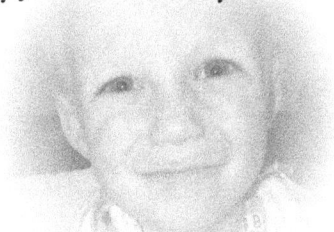

"THE WORLD BREAKS EVERYONE AND AFTERWARD

many are strong at the broken places."

— Ernest Hemingway

OUR SAWYER RYAN DEERMAN WAS BORN JUNE 22, 2004. This was one of the happiest days of our lives. Our first child! How amazing.

On June 24, 2004, the day we were set to come home with our little bundle of joy, our pediatrician heard a noise in Sawyer's heart and proceeded to run some tests. The doctors discovered that our son had a medium to large VSD (ventricular septal defect) of the heart, which is a large hole between two chambers in the heart. The hole allows air and blood to mix when they should not.

When they broke the news, our world seemed to come crashing down on us. We felt utter shock and disbelief. Though the instinct is to try and figure out why, eventually you learn these things just happen. The odds are that one out of 125 children will be born with some sort of heart defect.

The doctors at UAB wanted to do open-heart surgery right away to repair the hole because of its size. Having never heard of a VSD, we were terrified. I kept hearing the words "open heart surgery" and thinking, Why us? Why our child? Every thought crosses your mind, including death. Hearing something is wrong with your child is never easy, especially a life-threatening defect.

We began weekly visits to the cardiologist to monitor the hole. By the grace of God, it began to show signs of trying to close. Surgery was put off each visit, and this gave us a false since of security. These visits continued for the next two years.

On December 8, 2006, on one of our normal visits, Dr. Colvin, Sawyer's cardiologist at UAB, discovered that the VSD's location was now affecting his aortic valve, causing it to leak. The doctor decided that open-heart surgery was now necessary, to repair the hole and take the pressure off the valve to prevent it from leaking any more. Once again, our world crashed. I had been relying on the fact this problem was going away, and now it was back and staring my family right in the eye.

On January 1, 2007, we checked into UAB Hospital, in Birmingham, Alabama. No parent is ever prepared for this. I remember my husband and I lying on the floor beside our son's bed, crying and praying all night long. We found ourselves questioning the decision to have our child's heart repaired. At these times, it feels like everything you have has been taken away. The only thing you have that cannot be taken away is your faith in God and the belief that he will handle the situation.

On January 2nd, we carried our little boy all the way down to the surgery unit door and carefully placed him in the arms of a nurse. I asked the nurse for one favor. I said, "Please take care of my child and treat him as if he was yours."

Sawyer underwent open-heart surgery that day. They had to actually stop the heart, using a heart/lung bypass machine, and place a patch over the hole. Four hours felt like four years. Our child was lying on a table, having open-heart surgery, and the only thing we could do for him was WAIT and PRAY. I don't know which part was worse, waiting in anticipation of the surgery, or the actual day of the surgery. I just know they were both horrible.

We got to see Sawyer right after surgery, but our hearts were still breaking. Our child was lying in a bed with tubes and wires everywhere. He was so innocent and sweet, yet had just undergone a major surgery. He had been through more in two years than I will in my entire life. Children can be so strong.

Sawyer never once complained during, or after his surgery. Within two days, he was riding a bicycle down the halls of the fifth floor of the children's heart unit, at the hospital. We took turns running behind him, barely able to keep up. A few words to describe my feelings after Sawyer recovered from surgery; amazing, inspirational, and just plain beautiful.

Through all of this, one thing we learned is that you have to be tough, you have to have faith, and that God will always make the right decisions. Some stories do not end as happy as ours has. Some will.

Our son is better now, we are stronger as a family, and our faith is solid as a rock. You cannot let a bump in the road, no matter how serious, bring you down, or tear your family apart. You must educate yourself, your family, and your child. You have to support one another and take turns leaning on each other.

We didn't hide a single thing from Sawyer. We told him everything that was happening and what was going to happen next, even about the surgery. I believe we were given a special gift when God gave us our baby boy with a heart defect. I wouldn't change a thing if I could. Sawyer has a larger purpose in life. I'm not sure what God has in store for him, but I know that his heart won't slow him down.

After the surgery was over and Sawyer was out of CICU, the nurses brought him his Bravery Beads necklace. We'd seen the posters on the walls at the hospital. Sawyer was so excited to receive his necklace. He proudly put it around his neck. He received many different beads, one for each procedure he went through, and he went through a lot. The necklace brought a smile to my son's face, replacing the tears and sadness he'd been wearing.

The necklace is not just a necklace. It's a victory, an accomplishment—a token of hope, love and happiness. It represents more than words can describe. I am so proud of my son. At the age of 2 ½, he has endured more than most of us ever will. Sawyer is my child, my hero, and my life.

He is now in the process of recovering from his surgery.

He is expected to make a full recovery with no future complications. In December of 2008, we went back for another follow up visit. The leak could not be found in his heart, and the patch was still in place and looked great. A child is the most precious gift in the world. Thank you for giving my child a reason to smile.

PURCHASE THIS BEAUTIFUL

hand-made Bravery Heart Necklace

in support of our Bravery Beads Programs

*for $20.00 at **www.braveryhearts.com**.*

RESOURCES FOR PARENTS

CANCER

The Facts about Childhood Cancer

- ♥ Every day, 46 children and teens are diagnosed with cancer.
- ♥ 50,000 children and teens are battling childhood cancer inside hospitals today.
- ♥ 250,000 children are affected by childhood cancer today.
- ♥ Childhood cancer is the leading cause of death by disease in children and teens.

Best Resource—Kids Cancer Pages

National Childhood Cancer Resource Directory

This is the first comprehensive national resource guide for children and families battling childhood cancer. It provides hundreds of listings to help families make decisions about medical treatments and pain management, find information about financial aid and healthcare assistance, and discover resources that can bring peace and guidance to the child and family. Basically, it is a guide for the journey these children and families are embarking on.

CONTACT:

Children's Cancer Association

7524 SW Macadam, Suite B

Portland, OR 97219

Phone: 503-244-3141, Fax: 503-892-1922

Email: office@e-cca.org

Web: www.ChildrensCancerAssociation.org

Other Wonderful Resources

American Cancer Society

PROGRAMS:

- ♥ Rock Camp: Rock Camp is for kids ages 7-16 in active cancer treatment, or within three years post treatment, and referred by pediatric oncologist.
- ♥ Families ROCK Weekend: Families of children 17 years or younger who are newly diagnosed with cancer and referred by pediatric oncologist.
- ♥ College Scholarship: Must have personally experienced a cancer diagnosis, and are a Florida resident under age 21 at the time of application, and plan to attend an accredited Florida College.

CONTACT:

Susan Bellomy, mEd, CCLS

Director, Childhood Cancer Programs

American Cancer Society-Florida Division, Inc

3709 West Jetton Avenue

Tampa, FL 33629

Phone #: 813-349-4405, Fax #: 813-254-5857

Susan.Bellomy@cancer.org

Childhood Leukemia Foundation

PROGRAMS:

♥ Hope Binders include: Log for doctor names and numbers, treatment log, med log, appointment log, calendar, and pre-paid phone card. Come with six in a box.

♥ Wish Baskets: Baby (newborn to 2 years) infant robe, personal care products, educational materials, toys and a $50 gift card; Child (ages 3-10 years) PJ's with matching pillow case, personal care products, educational materials, games and/or toys, mp3 player; Teen (ages 11-21 years) PJ's with matching pillowcase, personal care products, educational materials, games, mp3 player (ipod) and a $50 gift card.

♥ Hugs U Wear: Cotton skullcap with real hair, choice of hair color, texture, color and cap. Must measure head circumference.** To authorize, put in (hugs).

♥ Authorization #: 37032192 for Hope Binders and Wish Baskets.

CONTACT:

Kate Booth, Program Services Director

Kim Wetmore, Director of Development

Childhood Leukemia Foundation

807 Mantoloking Rd.

Brick, NJ 08723

Phone #: 732-920-8860 or toll free: 1-888-253-7109

E-mail: kbooth@clf4kids.org or kwetmore@clf4kids.org

Website: www.clf4kids.org

First Hand Foundation

REQUIREMENTS:

- May apply for funding one time in a 12-month period, and no more than a total of three times to the foundation.
- Max assistance is $2,400.
- Reimbursement of 0.33 per mile and $10 a day per person for food.
- Max income of $42,000 per year for one child.
- Letter from doctor on letterhead explaining the child's diagnosis, history of illness, specific request for funding, and other relevant information.
- Letter from provider on letterhead showing the original cost and estimated discount (must have a discount for First Hand to assist).
- Copy of first page of Federal Income Tax return.
- Letter of denial from insurance company (if applicable).
- Child's photograph and photo release form.
- Must submit by the last Wednesday of the month to be reviewed by the Clinical Decision Committee meeting on the first Wednesday of the month.

- ♥ Case Manager will follow-up with applicant within a week of the meeting.
- ♥ If approved, funding sent to provider within two weeks. **This funding must be used within twelve months of the date granted.

PROVIDE ASSISTANCE FOR:

- ♥ Clinical Request Services: surgeries, clinic visits, procedures, therapy etc.
- ♥ Medication
- ♥ Equipment
- ♥ Displacement request for travel, food, lodging.

INFORMATION:

- ♥ Occupation of parent(s)/guardian(s).
- ♥ Annual household income.
- ♥ Type of insurance coverage.
- ♥ Out-of-pocket medical expenses in the last year for the candidate.
- ♥ Additional funding sources and amount.
- ♥ Type of treatment, number of treatments, cost per treatment, discount price,
- ♥ name and address for payment remittance.
- ♥ Medication name, number of months needed, cost per month, willingness of provider to work with First Hand regarding a discount, name and address for payment remittance.

♥ Equipment cost, discounted price, name and address for payment remittance.

♥ Displacement Request for Travel: purpose, transportation between cities, method of transportation, number of individuals, number of roundtrips, cost per adult, cost per child, estimated roundtrip mileage (if traveling by car), name and address for payment remittance; Displacement Food: number of individuals, number of days needed, hospital-provided assistance or voucher information, name and address for payment remittance; Displacement Lodging: number of individuals, number of nights, type of lodging, cost per night, option for charitable housing, discounted cost, name and address for payment remittance.

CONTACT INFO:

Nurse Case Manager

First Hand Foundation

2800 Rockcreek Parkway

Kansas City, MO 64117

Phone #: 816-201-1569

Fax #: 816-571-1569

E-mail: alexis.cole@cerner.com

Website: www.firsthandfoundation.org

Leukemia & Lymphoma Society

REQUIREMENTS:

- ♥ Must be a US resident.
- ♥ Must be in active treatment or ongoing medical follow-up for leukemia, lymphoma, myeloma, myelodysplastic syndromes or other blood cancers.
- ♥ MD must sign bottom of application.
- ♥ May fax form but must mail hard copy with original signatures.
- ♥ May reapply every year after June 30th.

ASSISTANCE PROVIDED:

- ♥ $100 per year.
- ♥ Financial aid program begins each July 1st and ends each June 30th .
- ♥ Must reapply every year after June 30th.

INFORMATION:

- ♥ Date of birth
- ♥ Date of diagnosis
- ♥ Ethnicity
- ♥ Health Insurance
- ♥ Prescription drug plan
- ♥ Medicare
- ♥ Medicaid
- ♥ Parent/Guardian signature
- ♥ MD signature

CONTACT INFORMATION:

Main Office Info:

Leukemia and Lymphoma Society of America

1311 Mamaroneck Ave

White Plains, NY 10605

Phone: 914-949-5213 or 800-955-4572

Fax: 914-949-6691

Web: www.leukemia.org

Local Chapter for West Palm Beach:

Sharon Cohan, LCSW

Patient Services Manager

The Leukemia & Lymphoma Society: Palm Beach Chapter

4360 Northlake Boulevard, Suite 109

Palm Beach Gardens, FL 33410

Phone #: 561-775-9954

Toll free #: 888-478-8550

Fax #: 561-775-0930

E-mail: Sharon.cohan@lls.org

National Children's Cancer Foundation:

REQUIREMENTS:

♥ Must be a US citizen.

♥ Must be diagnosed with a pediatric cancer or a high grade or anaplastic brain tumor.

♥ Must be diagnosed on or before his or her 18th birthday.

♥ Family must have liquid assets less than $5,000.

♥ Assistance may be requested for up to two months or 60 calendar days. Additional requests may be made in writing. A new application is only needed if length of time between requests has been over one year. Letter to include: child's full name, date of birth, diagnosis, past treatment info, plan of treatment for next 60 days, other community resources being used.

PROVIDE ASSISTANCE FOR:

♥ Meals during treatment.

♥ Transportation to and from treatment.

♥ Long distance phone cards.

♥ Lodging during treatment.

♥ Health Insurance premiums.

♥ Medical Expenses not covered by insurance: Bone Marrow Transplant, Donor Search, Donor Harvest, Pharmaceuticals/Supplies, other cancer treatment procedures (Will require: letter from physician detailing child's diagnosis, treatment history and recommended procedure, letter from hospital detailing all costs and hospital's official position on treating a patient without means to pay, letter of denial and a copy of the insurance policy may be requested if a procedure/

treatment is denied by Medicaid or a private insurance company.)

INFORMATION REQUIRED:

- ♥ Place of Birth (state/country).
- ♥ Child's S.S. number.
- ♥ Parents' marital status.
- ♥ Emergency contact number.
- ♥ Parent/Guardian Employer(s) & Salary (net annual).
- ♥ Other income: SSI, Child Support, FANF.
- ♥ Banking Accounts with account numbers (checking & savings).
- ♥ Copy of last statement of accounts.
- ♥ Info and value of money market, CD's, mutual funds, stocks & investments excluding IRAs and retirement accounts.
- ♥ Fundraising events and amount raised.
- ♥ Assistance from other organizations.
- ♥ Insurance info: name of plan, percent of coverage, address and phone number of company, information on assistance for meals, transportation or lodging, any secondary insurance or Medicaid.
- ♥ Parent(s)/Guardian(s) S.S. number.

MAIL OR FAX APPLICATION TO:

(fax#) 314-241-1996

The National Children's Cancer Society

Patient and Family Services

One South Memorial Drive, Suite 800

St. Louis, MO 63102

Super Sibs

REQUIREMENTS:

♥ Children 4-18 years who have a brother or sister diagnosed with cancer.

INFORMATION REQUIRED:

♥ Name, sex, birth date, and age of the siblings.

♥ Patient name, birth date, age, diagnosis, date of diagnosis, hospital, doctor name and phone.

♥ Parent(s)/Guardian(s) name(s), address, phone number, language, email address.

♥ Ethnicity

CONTACT INFORMATION:

SuperSibs

4300 Lincoln Ave., suite 1

Rolling Meadows, IL 60008

Phone: 847-462-4742

Toll Free: 866-444-7427

Fax: 847-984-9292

www.supersibs.org

Brain Tumor Foundation for Children, Inc.

REQUIREMENTS:

- ♥ Application must be typed and submitted by qualified medical personnel.
- ♥ For families of children and young adults with brain or spinal cord tumors.
- ♥ Bill payments are made directly to creditors on behalf of the family.
- ♥ Will pay: rent, mortgage, utilities, car loans & repairs, misc. household expenses which may not be able to afford due to loss, or decrease in income related to child's diagnosis and treatment.
- ♥ Items not covered by some health insurance plans: special meds, long-term rehab, hearing devices, wigs & prosthetic devices, home health services, tutoring, summer school.
- ♥ Travel & lodging expenses: hotel stays, grocery cards, gas cards, etc…associated with seeking and/or obtaining treatment.
- ♥ Funeral expenses.
- ♥ Limited to $2,000 per family per year as long as needed for the child's tumor diagnosis (year runs from time assistance is first offered).
- ♥ Must submit bills.

CONTACT INFO:

Sherry Samuels, Director of Patient & Family Services

Butterfly Funding Program

Brain Tumor foundation for Children

6065 Roswell Rd., Suite 505

Atlanta, GA 30328-4015

Phone: 404-252-4107

Fax: 404-252-4108

Email: sherry@braintumorkids.org

Cure Search

SERVICES OFFERED:

♥ Provides information specific to cancer type, treatment, stage and age group. Includes information regarding the risks and side effects of treatment, as well as life after treatment issues. Cure Search represents the combined efforts of the National Childhood Cancer Foundation (NCCF) and the Children's Oncology Group (COG)

CONTACT:

Cure Search

National Childhood Cancer Foundation (NCCF)

4600 East West Highway, #600

Bethesda, MD 20814-3457

Phone: 800-458-6223,

Fax: 301-718-0047

Email: info@NCCF.org

Web: www.curesearch.org

Candlelighter's Childhood Cancer Foundation

SERVICES OFFERED:

♥ National pediatric cancer foundation provides information, local support groups & specialized information to families & caregivers of children with cancer.

CONTACT:

Candlelighter's Childhood Cancer Foundation

PO Box 498

Kensington, MO 20895-0498

Phone: 800-366-2223

Email: staff@candlelighters.org

Web: www.candlelighters.org

Caring Bridge

SERVICES OFFERED:

♥ Free web page connecting patients with family and friends. A free service providing support and encouragement to families who are facing difficult times.

CONTACT:

Caring Bridge

3440 Federal Dr., Suite 100

Eagan, MN 55122

Phone: 651-452-7940, Fax: 509-351-5126

Web: www.caringbridge.org

Patient Advocate Foundation

PROGRAM:

♥ Provides legal consulting and referral services for patients confronting denial of insurance coverage, employment discrimination and/or the need for negotiating support with public assistance programs through both state and federal agencies through their national Legal Resource Network.

CONTACT:

Pamela Cleck

Director

Patient Advocate Foundation, Co-Pay Relief Program

700 Thimble Shoals Blvd., Suite 200

Newport News, VA 23606

Direct Dial: 757-952-1375, Direct Fax: 757-952-2469

Toll Free: 1-866-512-3861 x1134

Email Address: Pam.Cleck@patientadvocate.org

Website: www.patientadvocate.org, www.copays.org

United Healthcare Children's Foundation

PROGRAM:

♥ Grants that provide financial relief for families who have children with medical needs not covered or not fully covered by their commercial health benefit plan. The foundation aims to fill the gap between what medical services/items your child needs and what your commercial health benefit plan will pay for.

GRANT APPLICATION – CHECKLIST

♥ Your child's social security number.

♥ Name and policy number of your child's current commercial health benefit plan. Medicaid, Medicare, SCHIP (which may be called various names by each state), HIS or other state or federally subsidized health insurance programs given to those without insurance or with low incomes are not eligible.

♥ A description of your child's medical condition.

♥ A description of the treatment, therapy, etc. your child's doctor or other health care professional has specifically prescribed. You can list multiple items, if appropriate.

♥ The estimated total cost of the treatment, therapy, equipment or service.

♥ How much, if any, your insurance will help pay for.

♥ How much you will have to pay, after insurance.

♥ The child's primary care medical doctor (M.D. or D.O.) name, phone number and address.

♥ An outline of your finances - monthly income, monthly expenses and total assets (bank accounts, investments, 401(k), etc.).

♥ The Foundation will request that some paperwork be sent to us via mail at the end of the online application. We will ask for:

- A one-page letter from your child's primary care medical doctor (M.D. or D.O.) that clearly states the child's medical condition and recommended therapy, services, etc. is required. This letter must be from your child's M.D. or D.O. and must support what you are asking for in the application. If the M.D. or D.O. letter does not specifically support what you are asking for in the application, the items will not be considered. Therapist, specialist, etc. letters may be sent in, but will only be considered as supplementary information and not as a substitute for the required M.D. or D.O. letter.

- Your IRS 1040 from the previous tax year that specifically lists your child as a dependent.

- If you are requesting help with anything that your insurance company will not cover at all (0%), we will ask for proof.

♥ The Foundation may also request additional information from you after the application is submitted.

GRANT APPLICATION - CRITERIA

Please carefully read the criteria. Applications submitted that do not meet the criteria will not be considered. The Foundation may also request additional information from you after the application is submitted.

In evaluating applications, the Regional Board will consider applications based on the following criteria:

1. The following items are excluded from grant consideration: dental or orthodontic treatment unrelated to a serious medical condition, biomedical consultations, chelation therapy (this exclusion does not apply for a primary medical diagnosis of lead toxicity confirmed by blood lead levels), educational tutoring, heavy metal toxicity testing, herbal testing, home improvement/modifications, hyperbaric oxygen treatment, service dogs and other pets (does not apply to animals who support the visually impaired), camps, therapies of feeding, listening, vision, cognitive, neuro-feedback and social skills.

2. The applicant must be 16 years old or younger and live in the United States and receive and pay for care/items in the United States.

3. The applicant must be covered by a commercial health

benefit plan and limits for the requested service are either exceeded, or no coverage is available, and/or the copayments are a serious financial burden on the family. The United Healthcare Children's Foundation requires a commercial health benefit plan. A commercial health benefit plan is defined below:

INCLUDED:

♥ Your commercial health benefit plan is offered through:

- Your commercial (private) employer. Example: most grant applicants whose parent works for a commercial entity will have this type of health insurance.

- Your health benefit plan is offered through a commercial health plan that you individually purchased. Example: small business owners, sole-proprietors, etc.

- Your health benefit plan is offered through your employment with a town, city, state or federal government. Example: teachers, police officers, active duty or civilian military duty, etc.

EXCLUDED:

♥ Medicaid, Medicare, SCHIP (which may be called various names by each state), HIS or other state or federally subsidized health insurance programs given to those without insurance or with low incomes.

4. The potential of the intervention to significantly enhance either the clinical condition or the quality of life for the child, the financial status of the family and the severity of the child's illness. If a grant is approved, services must be provided by a trained, and if appropriate, licensed professional.

5. Financial need of the child's family will be evaluated and documented through information provided on the application and by submission of a photocopy of the most recently filed Federal tax return (Internal Revenue Service 1040, 1040-A, or 1040-EZ). The following scale will be used to determine financial eligibility:

   * Your Family Size as reported on your IRS 1040 and Adjusted Gross Income as reported on your IRS 1040

     2 - $40,000 OR LESS

     3 - $50,000 OR LESS

     4 - $60,000 OR LESS

     5 - $70,000 OR LESS

     6 - $80,000 OR LESS

     7 OR MORE - $90,000 OR LESS

6. Awards will NOT be granted to individuals in families whose Adjusted Gross Income (AGI) exceeds the scale.

7. Other financial resources to meet the health care need are not available.

8. The amount awarded to an individual, within a 12-month period, is limited to either $5,000 or 85% of the fund balance whichever amount is less. Awards to any one individual are limited to a lifetime maximum of $7,500.

9. An application must be submitted prior to the child's 17th birthday.

10. The health care professional is to be paid directly; exceptions can be made to reimburse the family if adequate documentation is submitted showing the health care professional has been paid.

11. Applications are to be reviewed by a health care professional appointed by the Foundation to determine the medical appropriateness of the treatment.

12. An application must be submitted to the Foundation prior to the receipt of services. The Foundation does not pay for past medical expenses.

13. Applicants who are not approved by the Regional Board must wait a period of twelve months before re-applying, unless the medical condition and requested items have significantly changed from the original request.

14. In order to apply for your child, the child must live with you 51% of the time, or more, and be listed as

a dependent on your most recently filed IRS 1040. If the child is not listed on your most recently filed IRS 1040, then we need a copy of both your most recently filed IRS 1040 and the most recently filed IRS 1040 on which the child is listed as a dependent.

15. If a grant is approved, you cannot re-apply for another grant until 30 days before your current grant expires. Yearly and lifetime maximum grant limits apply.

HEART INFORMATION

These resources on cardiac care and transplant were generously provided by Blair Couvillion.

Okay, here are my tips for families with children with congenital heart disease. Most of this information will also translate over to heart transplantation.

First, I would recommend that all parents make contact with their child life specialist for more advice specific to their hospital.

Next, I can offer a list of particularly helpful resources:

- ♥ *Thriving With Heart Disease* by Wayne Sotile. This book is written for adults and is a great book for parents to read.

- ♥ *It's My Heart* is a book put out by the American Heart Association, and it does a great job describing each congenital defect and the surgical repairs in a way non-medical minds can comprehend.

- ♥ *Heart Pro 3* is an app that shows different defects and procedures digitally, from different angles, and in 3D. It is great for those parents and patients that are visual learners!!!

I would encourage parents to see if their area has a Mended Little Hearts chapter and, if not, perhaps consider starting one! A wonderful support group for parents and patients with heart defects and heart transplants, it is part of an adult group called Mended Hearts.

There are some things I have found helpful for CHD families. First, if a baby is diagnosed in utero, I would encourage parents to contact the hospital and set up a prenatal tour. This way, the family can become familiar with the ICU and step-down unit before the baby is born. For expectant moms planning to breastfeed, be sure and ask questions in advance. This is a great way for a mom to gain some control during an out of control time in their lives. It helps moms to know that there is something they can do to help their baby.

If there are siblings, have them prepped for their visit with the child life specialist.

Also look into cardiac or transplant summer camps in your area. This is a great way to meet other families with whom you can potentially be lifelong friends and part of a support system.

Blair Couvillion, BS,CCLS
Child Life Department
Huntsville Hospital for Women and Children
911 Big Cove Road
Huntsville, AL 35801

March of Dimes

The mission of the March of Dimes is to improve the health of babies by preventing birth defects, premature birth, and infant mortality. Below is a list of March of Dimes websites:

- ♥ **marchofdimes.com** – The March of Dimes website contains information for individuals and health care professionals to help women have healthy pregnancies and healthy babies.

- ♥ **marchofdimes.com/nicu** – The March of Dimes NICU Families website contains information for parents, extended family, and friends who are dealing with the NICU hospitalization of a newborn.

- ♥ **shareyourstory.org** – This online community for NICU families is a place where families can connect with each other, share their stories, and participate in online discussions.

- ♥ **nacersano.org** – The March of Dimes Spanish-language website provides culturally relevant information for Spanish-speaking NICU families.

GET INVOLVED

You can support Bravery Beads and help us on our mission to put a Bravery Beads Program in every children's hospital in North American and beyond.

- ♥ Become a Bravery Hearts sales rep and sell our hip and trendy fashion accessories

- ♥ Make a donation to the Bravery Beads Foundation on our secure website at **www.braveryhearts.com**

- ♥ Sponsor a bravery beads program at your local children's hospital complete with a naming opportunity.

- ♥ Help spread the word about Bravery Hearts by sharing our facebook page with all your friends, **www.facebook. com/braveryhearts**

- ♥ Shop at **www.braveryhearts.com** where you will find hip and trendy fashion accessories, as well as funky and cool gifts, all sold in support of our Bravery Beads programs.

www.ingramcontent.com/pod-product-compliance
Lightning Source LLC
LaVergne TN
LVHW021459080426
835509LV00018B/2337